My Loving
Daddy

PATSY SECRIST

ISBN 978-1-0980-2678-3 (paperback)
ISBN 978-1-0980-2680-6 (hardcover)
ISBN 978-1-0980-2679-0 (digital)

Christian Faith Publishing, Inc.
832 Park Avenue
Meadville, PA 16335
www.christianfaithpublishing.com

Printed in the United States of America

The thief has only one thing in mind—he wants to steal, slaughter and destroy. But I have come to give you everything in abundance, more than you expect—life in its fullness until you overflow!

—John 10:10 (TPT)

Acknowledgments

I would like to acknowledge the following people who have touched my life in one way or another:

- My mama-san in Yokohama, Japan, who took care of me until I was four and taught me to love rice with soy sauce.
- Mrs. Bonner, my first-grade teacher in Gulf Breeze, Florida, who hugged me and apologized profusely when I wet my panties in class.
- My grade school teachers in Charleston, South Carolina, who felt great compassion for me when they saw how beaten I came to school every day.
- Wendy, the manager of Biff Burger in Charleston, South Carolina, who gave me my first job.
- Donald, my first "boyfriend," who gave his life for his country in Vietnam.
- Michael O'Brien, my first husband, who taught me that making love really was a good thing and gave me my baby girl, Jennifer Michelle.
- Jennifer Michelle O'Brien, my first child and only daughter. This little bundle of joy has always been first in my heart, and I love her so much I gave her the middle name *Michelle* from my favorite music group, the Beatles.
- Bruce Wilcox, who was my second husband. He gave me a crazy, hippy life and a son, Bruce Ozman. Oh, what a wonderful life we had!
- Bruce Ozman Wilcox, my second child and only son. The cutest little guy ever, and so much like me and his dad.

- Amy, the best friend of my life.
- Patricia Heubner, the college counselor at Eastern Idaho Technical College, who told me I was smart after I took the general education development tests.
- Wick, my "boyfriend," who was the best pool player I have ever seen.
- Kery Wyn Secrist, the love of my life, my husband and my best friend. I believe God put Kery in my life for a reason and a purpose—to love and care for me—and he has done a wonderful job
- Columbia Foursquare Church (CFC) in Richland, Washington. I have attended about five churches in thirty-five years, and none has made me feel more welcome and loved than this one.
- Jon and Candy, pastors at CFC, who were the best living examples of Jesus I have ever met. I can't say enough of what good people they both are.
- The lovely princesses of CFC who were part of our Wednesday-night ladies' Bible study: Candy, Karla, Danae, Mary, Irene, Laura, Nancy, Elaine, Terry, and many others.
- My cousins in Ohio—Carolyn, Joyce, Bobby, and Karen— who walked over the chicken line and called the stranger in Idaho.
- Jesus Christ, my Lord and Savior, who loved me first so I could love Him and have this abundant life.

Music

I have always loved music because it was always my escape from reality; it brought me comfort and soothed my spirit. I have identified with so many songs that describe a certain time in my life. I hope you will bear with me as I share the words of specific songs that have touched my life throughout this book.

Introduction

It was January 1951, and Harry S. Truman was the president of the United States when I was born at Garfield Memorial Hospital in Washington, DC.

Our family lived a few miles away on the other side of the Potomac River in Alexandria, Virginia. Mom and Daddy already had one child who had been born five years before in 1946—Charles Alvin Ward III. We called him Chip. Then came me in 1951, and five years later, in 1956, my baby brother was born, Stephen Edward Ward (Steve). He was named after my father's brother, Edward (Uncle Polo). Then two years later, my sister, Pamela Annette Ward (Pam), was born in 1958. We were the four children of Charles Alvin Ward Jr. and Elsie Janice (Dunn) Ward.

Daddy was the first to pass away in February 1976 from cirrhosis of the liver and heart failure. He was sixty years old. My older brother Chip died in 1992, when he was forty-five. It was from an accidental death at a hospital. My baby sister died of cancer in 1993, when she was thirty-three.

We all have our own stories, and one thing I know, life is not always perfect.

When I was nine years old, my father began to sexually abuse me, and that lasted until eighteen days before my thirteenth birthday. After that, he beat me with his belt buckle every day until I left home at fourteen.

But God shows up sometimes in the strangest places and strangest times. When I was twenty-seven, I was at the end of my third marriage and I was feeling like a complete failure. I had two kids from two different fathers and they were looking to me for stability. But when you have no faith in yourself and even though you're a mother of two you feel like a stupid, ugly child who will never amount to anything, a loser at life…obviously.

Then out of the blue, God shows up and tells me he loves me and that's all that matters! What? How can this be? But he offered me his hand and after a little initial shock, I took it and he helped me stand up in the coffin I had created.

The chains wrapped around me that held all the baggage were heavy and tight, suffocating sometimes. But I took the chance and asked him how to get rid of this heavy baggage and he said the simplest thing— love and forgive. What? Can it be that easy? And he just smiled.

Okay then, I will—love and forgive. And the craziest thing happens, the locks holding the chains tight click open and all the chains fall off and the baggage is now laying on the floor. If you were to peek inside some of the baggage you would see a furious abusive daddy in one, a complacent mother in another, three white supremacist girls in yet another. There were quite a few more but somehow, I knew not to open them up. I knew also that I had the responsibility to make a decision…to leave the baggage there or take it with me. It was relatively easy to leave most of them, but the ones with my mother and daddy were more difficult. They were my mother and father after all and I couldn't just leave them there and walk away. So, I picked those two up and took them with me. This turned out to be the wrong decision, again. I tried to deal with them at arm's length but that didn't work well. I knew I had to completely forgive and let it go. I knew I had to turn around and put it all behind me. God stood by me and gave me all the love and strength I needed to truly forgive. Then a life of healing, deliverance and wholeness began. It really was the strangest craziest thing.

Now he shows up when I run to scripture and it nurtures me in ways it never has before. He comes in a song, or in the moment you realize that beautiful sunrise or sunset is a gift from God! I'm so glad I was so crazy to begin with so I could see him.

When I was younger and didn't know better, I really thought I was the only girl in the world who had a father like mine, and I felt very alone. But I know better now. I know I was not alone, and you are not alone either. Many of us girls have had some sort of abuse we didn't deserve, so don't ever feel alone.

I wrote this because it helped me get it all out, and it is part of the healing process. My purpose and mission in life is to tell and write my story to help others, particularly to help you. God healed me completely, and today I live a very happy and victorious life—but only because of the grace and love of God.

I do a Bible study with my friends, and I read this one day in one of them. It is about stories, and it was written by Roselene Coblentz in a YouVersion Bible plan called "10 Habits of Intimacy with God."

> We all have stories. They all have labels: funny, sad, happy, pleasant, ugly, difficult, peaceful, silly, cute, painful, joyous, adventurous, hard, loving, unkind, exciting, hurtful, devastating, awesome, amazing, and the list goes on.
>
> So what do we do with all our stories? Sharing the delightful ones is always a blessing and remembering them can often bring even greater joy and pleasure. Then there are those painful ones that most of us want to put them into a dark, hiding place; ignore them in turning our backs on them; or dismiss them as though they never existed and hope they will just disappear like vapor or dissolve like ice, never to show their faces again.
>
> But sadly, stories don't work that way. We have been wounded and healing is needed, even if the story is from long ago. To heal, we have

to bring the story out of the dark and into the light. This usually is easier with a friend, mentor, or therapist alongside your journey. To choose a journey mate it is important that they are trustworthy and are committed to caring for your heart in the process. It is worthy to note that this is a two-fold journey: one, to return to the dark and retrieve your story and second, to bring them into the light to bring the healing desired. The two-fold journey is imperative to healing your heart and restoring your relationships whether that be God, you, others, or a combination. This journey is reflected in I Peter 5:10, "And the God of all grace, who called you to eternal glory in Christ, after you have suffered a little while, will himself restore you and make you strong, firm and steadfast." (NIV)

This is my story about how God took a broken and damaged little girl and gave her a new life. He truly is *my loving Daddy*.

"Wildflower," a song by Skylark

She's faced the hardest times you could imagine
And many times her eyes fought back the tears
And when her youthful world was about to fall in
Each time her slender shoulders bore the weight of all her fears
And a sorrow no one hears still rings in midnight silence, in her ears
Let her cry, for she's a lady
Let her dream, for she's a child
Let the rain fall down upon her
She's a free and gentle flower, growing wild
And if by chance I should hold her
Let me hold her for a time
But if allowed just one possession
I would pick her from the garden, to be mine
Be careful how you touch her, for she'll awaken
And sleep's the only freedom that she knows
And when you walk into her eyes, you won't believe
The way she's always paying for a debt she never owes
And a silent wind still blows that only she can hear and so she goes
Let her cry, for she's a lady
Let her dream, for she's a child
Let the rain fall down upon her
She's a free and gentle flower, growing wild
Let her cry, for she's a lady
Let her dream, for she's a child
Let the rain fall down upon her
She's a free and gentle flower, growing wild
She's a flower growing wild

Washington, DC, and Yokohama, Japan (1951–1955)

Mom and Daddy met and later married in Louisville, Kentucky, on December 21, 1945. She was a registered nurse, and he was in the US Army. He was a World War II veteran. The iconic picture of the navy guy kissing the nurse always reminded me of Mom and Daddy. Of course, it wasn't them, but it was a great picture that always reminded me of them.

Daddy wasn't there the day I was born, on that January day in 1951. He was off fighting a war in Korea. From her hospital bed, Mom wrote about me on the back of a postcard and sent it to her sister Edith Lyle in Dayton, Ohio. "She has brown hair and brown eyes, looks just like her daddy. Very sweet and cute. I am very happy with her. Just what I ordered." I read these words fifty-five years after they were written, when one of my cousins gave me a box of memorabilia of her mom's (Edith Lyle, mom's sister). Reading the words for the first time touched my heart and brought tears to my eyes. It took me way back to my younger days, when life was carefree and generally happy. Except thinking back now, I didn't remember her brushing my hair or holding me lovingly. I read the postcard and sat in bewilderment and wondered, when did she stop loving me? I searched my memories for any signs of her love and found none.

When I was six weeks old, our family moved from Alexandria, Virginia, to Yokohama, Japan, where we lived on a cliff overlooking the Pacific Ocean. I don't remember much, but my first memories were of a Japanese mama-san (nanny) who cared for me. I remember laughing and hanging from the seat in my little red eating table (a short table with a single seat hanging from a whole in the center). I ate pablum with milk and rice with soy sauce. I barely remember our large German shepherd dog named Mook. Mook had eight puppies, and when her pups were about eight weeks old, someone stole every single one of them during the night. I remember the Japanese policeman at our house and Daddy trying to tell them what happened in English. It wasn't very long after that when we moved back to the United States to Pensacola, Florida

Pensacola (Gulf Breeze),
Florida (1955–1960)

Daddy was born and raised in Pensacola, Florida, and because it was Daddy's hometown, it was mine too.

The beaches in Pensacola, Florida, are the best beaches in the world—beautiful sugar-white sand that squeaks when you walk through it and water that is baby blue and inviting. The sea oats sway in the warm breezes, and old wooden fences border the shoreline. It is gorgeous, and my memory holds that picture of white sand and blue water in my mind. I can almost feel the breezes when I close my eyes.

We lived in Gulf Breeze, which is just across the bay from Pensacola. Daddy was away in the army. Chip, Mom, and I spent our days on the white sands of the beaches. Chip and I spent hours upon hours next to the water, catching tadpoles, searching for sand dollars and shells, and building sandcastles.

Then I was old enough to learn how to swim. Chip was five years older than me and already knew how to swim, so he helped me learn. After mastering treading the water, it didn't take long before we were like fish in the sea. Swimming came natural for both of us. Where we swam was called the "sound," and I believe a sound is like a lake near the ocean or an inlet between two bodies of land. It is calm with gentle lapping waves, not the huge waves of the ocean. The water is easy to learn how to swim in, and we had no fear at all.

I can hear our giggles still—oh, what glorious days! While we played in and near the water, our mom loved to lie on a towel on the beach and read books. One thing I realized about Mom when I got older was that I love beaches today because she loved beaches.

Everywhere we lived, we were by the ocean; and I am thankful for her love of beaches because if she hadn't, I may not have found the joy of beaches in my own life. I also realized Daddy must have loved her to always buy her a house by a beach.

In July 1956, my baby brother, Stephen Edward, was born. I was five, and I was fascinated by this new baby. And he became my very own live baby doll. I loved holding him and taking care of him. He had big brown eyes, tan skin, and curly blond hair. He was adorable. One day when he was about six months old, I heard him crying in his crib. I automatically went in there to get him out. His body was almost as big as mine, and I struggled to get him out of the crib and into my arms. I carried him all the way through the house and into our kitchen, which had a swinging door. When Mom saw us coming through the swinging door, she was horrified to see Steve in my arms and the door swinging back toward us. She ran over to rescue him and took him out of my arms.

"Patsy, don't ever take him out of his crib again. Come get me, and I'll get him out for you," she warned me.

Chip and I were the babysitters while Mom worked. One day when Chip was eleven and I was six, I was making Steve's formula, which was made of Carnation evaporated milk and water. We used an ice pick to stab holes in the top of the Carnation milk can. I held the can with my left hand and the ice pick in my right, and as I was stabbing the can, the ice pick missed the can and went right through the flesh nearest the can on my left hand. I ran crying and screaming into the living room. "Chip, Chip!" I cried. "I stabbed my hand! Help me!" The ice pick was still protruding from my hand.

Chip calmed me down. "Hold on," he said. "I'll get it out." He grabbed the ice pick and pulled it out quickly. It was barely bleeding, but he took me into the kitchen and held my hand under cold water until it felt better.

When Mom got home, I showed her the hole in my hand. "Look what I did, Mommy." I pouted. She saw the hole in my hand, and being a nurse, she put antibiotic ointment on it and wrapped my hand with a bandage.

Chip always took care of me, but he liked to tease me too. One day we were home alone, and he found a gun in the house and started chasing me, saying, "Run, Patsy, run. I'm going to shoot you!" Where he found the gun, I don't know; but I remember being terrified and running around the house screaming, trying to get away from him. He waved the gun in the air and pointed it at me as he chased me through the house. I finally ran outside, and he didn't follow me. I never told Mom what he had done. I think about that today, and it's a wonder he didn't accidently shoot me.

Mom finally realized we were not such great babysitters, so that was when Barry came into our lives. I am not sure who "Barry" really was to our family, but we were told he was our godfather. I had a few memories of Barry. He was old, tall, and his shoulders were a little bent over, and he used to drink an entire ten-ounce Pepsi all at once.

One day, Barry took me to his brother's funeral, and I got my first lesson on dead people. His brother lay in the coffin in the front of the church, and Barry held my hand as we walked up the aisle to the front of the church and looked into the casket. His brother's dead body was barely a foot away from my face, and I stared at his unmoving white face for a few minutes and then asked Barry, "What's wrong with him?"

Barry told me, "He isn't breathing or alive anymore."

I didn't understand at first, but when the realization hit me, I backed away from the casket. My heart started beating wildly, and I started to cry. I had never seen a dead person and really never even thought about what it meant to be dead.

Barry got down on one knee and tried to console me and explain, "It's okay. He's in heaven now."

I didn't want to know anything more about it right then and there. "I just want to go home now. Can we go home now, please?"

He got up and took my hand, and we left the church. To this day, I don't like going to a funeral and looking at dead people.

In the fall, Chip went off to school, and I felt like I was losing my best friend. I remember standing in between the curtain and the big picture windows in front, watching him get onto the big yellow school bus. "I want to go to school too. Can I go with him?" I cried.

I remember Mom telling me, "He will be home soon."

But I didn't want him to leave me, and I whimpered all day long.

This was really when my love of music began because all day long, while Mom cleaned house and did the ironing, I was alone and lonely without Chip. Santa Claus had given me a record player the last Christmas we had, and it was pink and part of a box that closed like a little suitcase. And I carried it around with love. We had a blue curved sectional couch, and the space it provided in the corner of the room was big enough for me to take my record player, a blanket, and my favorite stuffed animal and listen to my records—78s and 45s, and mostly my mom's movie music records. But the music I loved the most at the time was Elvis Presley, Jim Reeves, and Marty Robbins.

I felt very secure and secluded behind the couch. It was like a secret hiding place, and the music brought me comfort, and it soothed my little soul. I lay on the floor looking up at the ceiling, and if I closed my eyes and listened to the words, I could imagine the stories they told. I love music to this day, and there are so many songs I have identified with through the years of my life. And they have become a part of who I am.

In Gulf Breeze, a family moved in behind us, and they had a daughter my age. Her name was Ann Gale Eddington. We became friends, and we played outside together most days. We rode our bikes to the beach because it was so close. We played in the forest between our houses and climbed big pine trees. One tree we saw had an eagle nest in it, but we never got that high in the tree.

We played in the sand hills behind our house. One Easter, Mom bought all us kids brand-new outfits and shoes to wear to church. I remember begging her to let me wear my brand-new black patent leathers out to play. When she gave in, Ann Gale and I headed back to the sand hills, and somehow I lost one of my shoes deep in the sandpile. Once I realized I had lost my shoe, Ann Gale and I dug through the sand furiously but couldn't find it. I ran home, crying and thinking Mom would come help me look for it or just buy me new ones. I told her, "Mommy, I lost one of my new shoes."

She only got angry with me. "Get back out there and find your shoe right now!"

I went back outside dirty and crying and went to the sand hill and started digging again, but still I couldn't find it. I hated having to go back inside and tell her I couldn't find my shoe, and I didn't know what to do. But I finally had to go inside, and she told me how angry she was at me for losing my shoe and spanked me and sent me to bed. I was very hurt that she had been so upset because I really wanted her to think of me as a good girl and cried myself to sleep. Needless to say, I didn't have new shoes for Easter Sunday.

Generally, life when I was young was quite carefree, and I was happy. Gulf Breeze, Florida, was warm and sunny, and I remember all the fun things we did—playing outside all day long until the sun went down.

Quite a few times in the summertime, the DDT (dichlorodiphenyltrichloroethane) truck would roll through our neighborhood, to kill the mosquitoes, sometimes two to three times per week. Chip and I looked forward to it, and when we heard it coming, we would run outside and jump on our bikes and follow it through the neighborhood. Other kids would join in, and soon we had a parade of kids laughing and riding in the fog of the DDT truck. No one stopped us kids even though it was toxic poison we were breathing!

We had a new house right on Fairpoint Drive, which was the main street going into Gulf Breeze. The yards were spotty with grass. It was mostly sand, but Mom had planted some gardenias and gladiolas—and they were always so colorful. She also had some rose bushes. We spent a lot of time out there in the yard pulling weeds; that was our job when we had to work for Mom, and we hated it.

Daddy was gone when I started first grade. Ann Gale, Chip and I rode our bikes to school every day. I felt so grown up now that I was going to school and going to my own class. Chip met Ann Gale and I after school, and we rode our bikes home together in the Florida sunshine.

Mrs. Bonner was my first-grade teacher, and I loved her. She was heavyset and had a large chest, which made her very motherly to us little kids. And she showed great patience to all of us first graders. One day I had to go "number one" pretty bad, and I asked Mrs. Bonner if I could go. She told me I had to wait for recess. I wiggled in my chair, trying to hold it in. My desk had an attached chair to it that had two scooped-out parts where your butt should fit.

In my young mind, I thought to myself, *If I just go a little bit, it will only fill the scooped-out parts of my seat.* So I let it go. The next thing I knew, Tony, a little boy who sat behind me, started yelling, "Patsy wet her pants! Patsy wet her pants!"

The whole class was looking at me, many of the kids laughing at my predicament. I looked down in horror to see the whole floor covered in yellow liquid. Mrs. Bonner ordered them to quiet down as she rushed to my side. After quickly assessing the situation, she took me to the bathroom; and as she helped me clean up and put my wet panties into a paper bag, she said, "Oh, Patsy, honey, I am so sorry. I am so sorry."

I was sobbing, and she had tears in her own eyes. She hugged me before she sent me home for the day. I got on my bicycle with my wet paper bag and rode all the way home alone. I hid the bag in the back of my closet and changed my clothes. Chip and Ann Gale rode home without me, and Chip yelled at me for leaving without them. I did not want to tell him I had wet my panties but had to in order to explain.

I was so embarrassed, but the next day, it seemed like it had been quickly forgotten. It was just like any other day—no one seemed to remember the horrible event that had happened to me the day before, and I was thankful.

We had a boxer dog named Ginger who was a great family dog. She loved to play, and we chased each other around the yard. She was very smart too and pretty. Her dark-brown eyes were like velvet. Her life ended the day she saved two-year-old Steve when she pushed him out of the road and got hit herself by a big truck going by. We were all heartbroken to lose our dog who had really been our friend. I remember Mom coming to get us out of school so we could go bury Ginger and have a little ceremony. Mom, Chip, Steve, and I dug a hole in our backyard, and we all stood there holding hands and looking at the covered-up hole in the ground where Ginger lay. And we cried together.

I had a strange fascination with fire for a short time when I was young for some reason. The woods were right next to our house, and I loved playing in it with my friend Ann Gale or alone. One day, I accidently caught the woods on fire. I just wanted to make a little campfire for myself. I had no intention of setting the forest on fire. I gathered some dried pine needles and some Spanish moss and padded them together on the ground. I found kitchen matches in the house and brought the whole box of matches with me. I had to learn how to strike a match, so I took one and struck it lightly on the box—nothing. I did it harder and harder until I finally got a flame, which scared me, and I threw it down, and it went out. I got out another match and struck it hard again, and this time, it didn't scare me. I held it to my little pile of fire starter, and it took right away. It wasn't long before it was smoking quite a bit, enough to make my eyes water.

While I was wiping my eyes, a little flame started, and I watched it out of my one open eye. Then the little fire started to spread pretty quickly in all directions, and it scared me. I tried to control it by stomping on the little flicks of flames with my *zori* (Japanese name for flip-flops) but couldn't get them all, and then I was afraid of burning myself. That's when I realized the fire was out of control. There was smoking Spanish moss everywhere, and I ran home before I got trapped in the burning woods. Standing on the grass of my yard and looking into the forest, I didn't see much; but the farther I got closer to the house, the more I could see smoke rising up.

Barry was watching us that day, and I knew I would be in deep trouble if I told him what I had done. My fear kept me from telling him about the fire. It wasn't long before I heard the sirens of the fire trucks, and Barry, Chip, and I went outside to see what was going on. I knew it was wrong to lie, but I lied that day when I stood there, watching the woods on fire, and said nothing.

Daddy came home six months later. Daddy was always funny and made us laugh, so when he was home, life seemed a lot better. And we were more like a complete family. Mom struggled while Daddy was gone, living as a single mom, taking care of four kids, and working full-time as a registered nurse. We were all really excited and happy when Daddy came home.

Daddy was a smoker and smoked nonfiltered Pall Malls. He would balance a cigarette in between his fingers with the lit side out; then he would slap the hand with his other hand, and the cigarette would fly in the air. He would catch it in his mouth, hopefully burning side out. We laughed so hard it made our tummies hurt, but we wanted him to do it again and again. He was very entertaining to us kids when we were younger.

Mom wasn't a very good cook, so Daddy was the main cook in our house. He made great spaghetti and chili, and that was what we usually ate, but he also knew how to catch crab off the bridge. We had a freezer full of cooked crab, and we ate crab fixed every kind of way you can imagine.

While Daddy was home, we went to our granddaddy's house in Pensacola. Granddaddy was my daddy's father, so he was Charles Alvin Ward Sr., and Daddy was Charles Alvin Ward Jr. I had never met my granddaddy before, and we only went to his house this once. I was about seven years old. I remember he came out of the house, and we met up on the porch. There was a chair on the front porch that he sat down in, and he took me up on his lap and looked into my green eyes. He seemed kind as he nuzzled my neck with his scruffy nonshaved face, and I giggled at his nuzzling, which I am sure tickled him too. We went into his house and straight back to his backyard, and to my surprise and delight, his backyard was full of pomegranate trees. He got one of the pomegranates off the tree, took out his pocketknife, and cut it open and gave each of us a piece. I tasted the sweet, tart seeds of the fruit, and I shivered from the tartness.

Daddy talked to his father as we squealed and chased each other around the trees in his backyard. We didn't stay long at his house, and he hugged us tight as we left, as if he would never see us again. I didn't know at the time he would be dead in less than a year. To me, it was a wonderful thing to meet any of our extended family. In my whole life, I don't remember ever meeting any of my mom's family and only my granddaddy on my dad's side. I never saw him again after that.

Tokorozawa, Japan, and Navy Housing (1960–1963)

In August 1958, my sister, Pamela Annette, was born into our family. Pam was a pretty baby and an even cuter little girl with dark-brown eyes and blonde hair. She and my little brother looked alike and were only two years apart, and they played together endlessly.

When Pam was about two, Daddy's work took us to Japan again. This time, to a little town called Tokorozawa. The house he found in Tokorozawa was tiny and had rice-paper dividers. I think the walls were made of rice paper too. It was so cold in that house that Chip and I used to get dressed for school in front of a small electric heater on the floor. We would shiver as we hurried to get our clothes on for the day.

There was a concrete fence in the backyard that was about six feet high and about one foot thick, and it separated us from a farmer's field. Chip and I climbed up on the wall occasionally, and one day, we watched as the farmer carried a pole with a bucket on each end on his shoulders. We watched him walk down the rows of his field, tipping the buckets, and a brown liquid poured from each bucket onto the field rows. It was a horrible smell, and it didn't take much to figure out what it was he was pouring on the plants—manure of some kind for sure. As we were living so close, it was a smell we had to endure every day.

I was always afraid of falling over the fence onto the farmer's side because the wall seemed to have no end; it curved around the neighborhood as far as I could see. If I fell, I had no idea how to get around the fence. It seemed like it was full of poop, and I did not want to fall.

Another day, Chip and I were riding our bicycles down a dirt path when a Japanese man came up behind us, riding his bicycle and ringing his bell at us. We stopped and let him go by us, and as he passed, we saw a big wooden box about six feet long strapped sideways on the back of his bike. The box was so wide it almost took up the whole path. We watched him pedal his bicycle down the lane, and once we knew he was out of sight, we followed him. We hid in the bushes as we watched him slide the wooden box into a small side door of a brick structure. He went inside, and very soon, there was smoke coming from a chimney on top. And we realized he was burning the box. Chip figured it out pretty quickly and told me the box was a coffin and there must be a body in the coffin. The realization frightened us, and we jumped on our bikes and rode home as fast as we could. We didn't want the Japanese man to see that we had followed him and that we saw him burning a body; it was just too weird.

At our house in Tokorozawa, I almost got run over while I was sleeping. I bet you have never heard that before! Our next-door neighbor allowed his son, a youngster of about twelve years old, to go out and start the car each day. Normally, the car must have been in park, but this day, it was either in reverse, or the kid put it in reverse. And when the car started, it went backward. And he must have pushed on the gas instead of the brake because the car swung around, and the rear end crashed into our house, right into my bedroom. I was still in bed, and it scared me to death as I was shocked awake with a car right next to my bed. My parents ran into my bedroom and found me screaming in my bed and were just as surprised to find a car in my bedroom. I was still in my pajamas, when the next thing I knew, the boy's parents were in my bedroom, they and my parents were yelling at one another. All I can say is that the Lord was watching out for me.

This event caused us to abandon the house in Tokorozawa, and we moved to military housing on the base. It was very much like today's condos. There were four "houses" in each building, and ours was the far right of the building from the road. Our building was the last one on the right before exiting the base near the back-gate exit.

Our family started going to an Episcopal church there on the military base. I learned a little about God and Jesus, and I actually got "confirmed" into the Episcopal church by memorizing some scripture. I think it had to do with being baptized in the church. We attended this church for the entire time we lived in military housing. I also remember going to a Catholic church with a friend, and the only reason I went with her was because I had a crush on her brother. He was a thirteen-year-old dreamboat.

By now, I was nine years old, and living in Tokorozawa taught me about the Japanese people so they didn't scare me. I used to go outside the security gate by myself and go to a little Japanese café that sold soba noodles in a delicious broth (much like ramen noodles but better). The owners and the patrons of the café were amazed to see a young towheaded green-eyed American child by herself in this little village café ordering soba. They delighted in me and chattered to one another in Japanese as they served me noodles.

Nine Years Old

It was at this time when my carefree/happy life came to an end. My life changed forever. One night, as I went to bed, it was storming outside. The clouds thundered, and the lightning was striking everywhere. And when a flash of lightning hit right outside my window, it scared me to death. I thought it was going to come right into my room. I jumped out of bed and ran through the adjoining bathroom to my parents' bedroom. I climbed into my parents' big bed on Daddy's side. He was warm, and I snuggled in next to him like a little spoon and felt safe from the storm that was going on outside. I took a few deep breaths, settled down, and was almost asleep when Daddy's arm moved over me. He put his hand on my belly and turned me over onto my back. I woke up a little, and at first, it felt more secure, and I had no reason to feel frightened. When I settled in again, I felt his hand starting to gradually gather up my nightgown, and he inched it up slowly and bunched it together near my belly. I remember wondering what he was doing, and my heart started beating wildly. And for some reason, I just froze in place. He put his hand inside my panties and slid his hand down my belly, and I stopped breathing. Alligator tears welled up in my eyes as his finger found my private parts, and I lay there on my back, eyes wide open in the dark, tears falling down the sides of my face. I felt him inside of me and pressing against me, and I almost threw up. I didn't know what to do. I was afraid to move. I was confused, and my mind was racing as I lay there in the dark. He finally took his hand out of my panties and rolled over. He left my nightgown bunched up, and I didn't move an inch until I heard him breathing deeply, and I figured he was asleep.

Ever so slowly, I got out of the bed and tiptoed to my own room and the safety of my own bed. I lay there wide awake and staring up at the black ceiling with hot tears running down the sides of my face, trying to figure out what had just happened. It was still thundering and lightning outside, and my insides hurt from his touch. I felt sick to my stomach, confused, hurt, and injured. I didn't know what to do. My mind could not process what had just happened, and I searched for a reason why. The only thing I could think of was that he must have thought I was my mom. I needed a why, and that was the best one I could think of. And I thought to myself, *I could even forget it happened if it was just an accident.* I loved my daddy, and he had never done anything like this before. No one had—ever.

The main bathroom to the house was down the hallway, and I tiptoed in and quietly shut the door before I turned on the light. I pulled my panties down and sat down on the toilet. And to my horror, my panties had a little bit of blood on them, and it scared me. What had he done? I didn't know what to do or what to think. I was obviously injured, but I didn't know who I could tell. Should I go wake up my mom? What would I tell her? What if it was just an accident? I was so confused. All I could do was cry silently. My innocent young mind could not fathom why he would want to do that to me. I took my panties off and hid them in the back of my closet and found clean ones in my drawer. I got into my bed and listened to the falling rain. I curled up with my stuffed dog, held on tight, and finally drifted off to sleep.

The next morning, I didn't know how to act or what to say. I was glad Daddy was gone already. I was tempted to tell Mom, but she was busy getting breakfast for me, my brothers, and sister. I didn't know how to tell her what had happened, and I didn't want my brothers or sister to hear either. I didn't know how she would react, or if she would even believe me, so I kept quiet. We sat at the big wooden dining table, and I silently ate breakfast. I was completely confused and didn't know what to do.

Then it was time to go to school, so I went outside with my older brother. And we got on the bus that took us to the military school on base. I couldn't stop thinking about what had happened and dreaded going home from school and the thought of Daddy coming home because I didn't want to face him. I didn't know what to say. After school, I kept to myself and stayed outside as long as I could. I saw Daddy's car drive up, and my heart fell like a rock into my stomach. But when I finally went inside, Daddy was acting like nothing had happened. I was relieved, and I too pretended nothing had happened. And the evening went on just like normal, and finally it was time to go to bed.

Lying in my bed, I told myself surely and hopefully, it must have been a mistake, and now it was over. Maybe he didn't realize he had done that to me, and it would never happen again. I had convinced myself it was just a mistake. I gave him the benefit of the doubt and made my decision—he must have thought I was Mom when he was touching me, and it was nothing more than that.

The next week, everything was somewhat back to normal in our house, but I wasn't able to put the incident completely behind me as if it never happened, but I tried.

It was just about a week later when the horrible, ugly truth became evident. I was asleep one night when I woke up feeling someone slipping into my single bed, next to me, and I immediately knew it was him because I could smell his Old Spice. I pretended to be asleep, and he pretty much repeated what he had done before. He left my bed, and this time, I knew he wasn't mistaking me for my mom. This time, I knew it was not an accident. My tummy was tied into knots, and my insides again were hurting by his rough hands. I didn't know what to do; the hot tears fell down the sides of my face as the truth hit me like a ton of bricks—it wasn't a mistake. I felt sick all of a sudden, and I ran to the bathroom to throw up my dinner.

His visits in the middle of the night became a regular occurrence, and I dreaded going to bed every night because I didn't know when he was going to be back. I don't know why, but for some reason, I did not want him to know that I knew. It seemed to me if I was awake, it would mean I accepted his actions; but if I pretended to be asleep, it was his doing and not mine.

It had gone on for so long I didn't feel safe telling Mom. She would want to know why I didn't tell her before, and I knew she wouldn't believe me now. I was embarrassed and felt ashamed because I never said no, so it was like I was allowing him to do this to me. I felt trapped because of my silence, but each time I wanted to scream, "No, don't!" But I couldn't. Why? I honestly don't know. I just knew I was full of shame and couldn't tell anyone.

I started to blame myself and thought I must be doing something that was attracting him to me, and I started wondering what was wrong with me. I was only nine years old, so I really couldn't comprehend why Daddy was doing this to me. And I don't know why I was trying to blame it on myself and take the blame off Daddy. Maybe it was because I wanted him to be Daddy, not this sex man. But now he scared and intimidated me, and he had a command over me that I didn't know how to stop. He knew what he was doing but acted like it wasn't happening. He would smile at me, and I would shrink. He wasn't the daddy that made me laugh and giggle anymore.

Normally, he repeated the same thing each time, until one night he actually went further. He pulled up my nightgown and pulled my panties all the way off, and without lying on top of me, he held himself above me and inserted himself inside of me. I whimpered in pain in my "sleep" and lay there in the dark, tears silently flowing down the sides of my face. I hated him and felt ashamed of myself for letting him do it. It hurt terribly, but I tried my best to keep quiet so he would not know I was awake.

The next morning, there was blood all over the bed under me. I remembered what I thought when I saw the blood. It was like "new evidence" of what Daddy was doing and decided it was time to tell Mom. This was the first time he had penetrated me, so I thought I could pretend this was the first time of everything. Just look what he did to me! I would tell my mom.

I called her into my bedroom and showed her the blood, and she automatically assumed I had started my period. Before I could say anything else, she called Daddy to my bedroom and told him to go to the store to get me some Kotex and a Kotex belt. I was completely shocked and embarrassed as he looked at the bloody bed, and I didn't know what to do. This had backfired on me and didn't turn out the way I had planned it.

Daddy went to the store, and they left me with a huge blue box of Kotex pads and a little belt that held the Kotex in place. Ironically, there I was, so young, and I had actually started my period.

My life changed. I was alone and didn't have any friends. I felt like I was damaged, worthless, and being used. I had secrets inside me I couldn't tell, so I withdrew and trusted no one. I struggled with what was going on and all my mixed emotions—blaming Daddy, and then blaming myself, then blaming Mom. My heart was sick and sad that I didn't have a daddy anymore. How could Mom not know what was going on?

Our family was still living in Japan, and I didn't know anyone that could help me or even how to get help. I was stuck in this cycle of abuse and didn't know how to get out of it. Every day I went to school, came home, and stayed outside until dinnertime. And I dreaded bedtime. Daddy made his way into my bed often, and it wasn't any particular day; it was any day of the week. Sometimes he would go a whole month before he snuck in again, but I went to bed troubled, expecting him every night.

I had bad dreams of him coming into my bed. Sometimes in my dreams, my bed would fall through the floor into a fiery pit. I remember waking up and having the feeling of falling. Other dreams were of Daddy using sharp knives to open up my privates, like Edward Scissorhands. I lay there screaming at the thought of him cutting me open. I also dreamed good dreams of running away forever and living in the sunshine on a beach all by myself.

In his attempt to act normal during the day, Daddy took Chip and me to Mount Fuji to climb its gentle slopes. We each got a thick beveled wooden walking stick. Mount Fuji had stations that you stopped at along the way up, and at each station, you could get your walking stick branded with the station you made it to. At the end, you have a walking stick with ten stations burned onto it. We started at the fifth station because you can drive to it. Reaching the summit, we were able to see forever from the top, and Japan was beautiful, although when you looked into the crater, it was filled with soda cans and trash. When we were ready to go down, we slid down a rocky, sandy slope, almost all the way down. It was an experience I will never forget.

I went into fifth grade, and my teacher was Mr. Travers. He was French and tried to teach us some of the French language. He introduced a few words each day, but I couldn't focus on memorizing the words and really lost interest. What I found most helpful was recess and playing tether ball. I loved knocking that ball around the pole. I seemed to be the champion—the benefits of being tall and angry, I guess. The release of tensions I got when I could knock the ball around the pole completely before the other girl could even touch it was quite satisfying. Tether ball was a one-against-one sport, and that was the way I liked it. I didn't have much going for me, but I was good at tether ball, and that made me feel some self-worth.

I also loved to run and swim, so I joined track in school, and I joined the swim team and excelled at swimming and won quite a few races. These extracurricular activities helped me realize I was good at some things, and my accomplishments started to build my self-esteem.

Salt Lake City, Utah (1963–1964)

We left Japan in 1963, when I was twelve years old. Daddy had left earlier for the United States to find a house for us. Mom took all four of us kids across the ocean in a passenger ship that took almost thirty days to get to San Francisco, California. It was glorious not to have Daddy around to worry about. My only "problem" was that Chip would not let me enter the "teen room" because I wasn't thirteen yet. I spent my time playing in the pool with Pam and Steve and lying in the chaise lounges on the front deck reading my books with Mom. I had just recently started to love reading, and my favorite was mysteries. I read every Nancy Drew book I could get my hands on. Music and now reading took me to a different place and brought me great comfort and freedom to dream.

We had a one-day stop in Kodiak, Alaska, and all the passengers got off the ship. We milled around the small town browsing the stores. Mom bought me a small Eskimo doll—she had on a white leather dress covered with colored beads, and she had long black braided hair. I treasured the gift because Mom didn't buy me gifts very often.

When we arrived in San Francisco, we boarded a passenger train that took us all the way to Chicago, Illinois. We had a one-room cabin with bunk beds on each side, and all of us slept in this room as we zipped across the countryside of the United States. We only made a few stops along the way. The dinners were served in the dining car by a male waiter dressed in a suit and a napkin draped over his arm.

This was the first time Mom ordered coffee for all of us. Chip was seventeen, I was twelve, Steve was nine, and Pam was seven. Mom told the waiter to bring five coffees. He looked around at us and said, "Madam, I'm sorry, but you can't give coffee to children."

She said, "I most certainly can. Bring coffee for all of us!"

He didn't quite know what to say, so he brought five coffees, and we all sat drinking our coffee from the small fancy coffee cups on saucers. Of course, it was mainly cream and sugar flavored with coffee, but we felt very grown-up. And we thought our mom was cool for letting us have coffee.

When we arrived in Chicago, we were to meet Daddy there so we could travel by vehicle down to Utah. But he wasn't there yet, so we went to a movie theater and watched my very first movie. It was called *Pollyanna* with Hayley Mills, and I fell in love with her and movies. Pollyanna became my hero and made me want to have a life just like hers, but it also made me realize just how dysfunctional my own life was. She was beautiful, and though she had unfortunate things happening to her, she was very positive and always happy. I wasn't anything like Pollyanna, but I wanted to be.

We checked into a big fancy hotel and waited for Daddy to arrive. Waiters brought up food when we were hungry, and I pretended like we were rich. And I tried to imitate Pollyanna, holding my cup with my little finger in the air.

Finally, there he was, knocking on the door, and I knew my days of freedom were over. We packed up our stuff and got into the car—a very large turquoise-blue Ford LTD. All four of us kids were in the back seat, and we traveled by car all the way to Salt Lake City, Utah. I would put my head on Chip's lap, and he would put his head down on my back. And that was how we took our naps. We stopped at hotels along the way, and it was a fun trip.

Daddy had arrived more than a month earlier and had rented a big house in downtown Salt Lake City, and we lived there for a few months. We were enrolled into school; I was put into sixth grade. One day, the loudspeakers at school announced that President Kennedy had been shot. It was November 1963. We were released early, and we all walked home from school very quietly. And when I got home, both of my parents were home watching the big black-and-white television, and they explained to us what had happened. It was a sad day for America, and my parents were both deeply moved. I was sad too, even though I didn't fully understand the importance of what had happened. I remember watching the videos over and over of him being shot and his wife trying to climb out of the back of the convertible car they were in.

Later on, we moved to a house in Murray, Utah, which was on the outskirts of Salt Lake City. We had our furniture from Japan moved into this new house. It was a split-level house with a kitchen, living room, and dining room on the middle level, a finished bedroom in a mostly unfinished basement for Chip, and an upper level with three bedrooms and two bathrooms for the rest of us kids and our parents. My bedroom was the last room on the left, and my parents' room was the last room on the right. And we had closets that were back to back.

Eighteen Days before
My Thirteenth Birthday

It was New Year's Day, 1964, eighteen days before my thirteenth birthday; and my mom, being a nurse on night shift, was still sleeping. All my siblings were out playing in the Utah snow, and I was sitting in the living room, watching television, when Daddy called me up to my bedroom in the middle of the day. I went upstairs and found him in my bed. He was under the covers bare-chested, and I assumed he was naked. He told me to shut the bedroom door and to come sit on the bed. I didn't want to, but I shut the door and sat down at the foot of the bed. Then he told me to sit closer and patted the bed next to him, then said, "But before you do, close the closet door so your mother doesn't hear us." My heart was racing, and I was scared and shaking. But I knew I had to take advantage of the situation. This was the first time I was wide awake, and I knew I couldn't let this happen. This was my first chance to say no, and I knew I had to do it.

I got up to close the closet door, and instead of going back to the bed, I jolted for the bedroom door and ran down the stairs. I grabbed my coat and ran out the door before he had a chance to even put his pants on to chase me. I ran down the street until I found Chip, who was with Steve and Pam, and they were sledding down the hill. I grabbed Chip frantically and told him Daddy might be coming after me. I had to tell him what had just happened; then I had to tell him about everything that had gone on since I was nine years old.

I could see the anger rising in his face, and he was ready to kill Daddy for what he had done to me, but also what he had done to him. Daddy had found pleasure in fist fighting with Chip and beating him to a pulp as much as he had enjoyed molesting me. This information about what he had been doing to me infuriated him and just added fuel to his anger. We left the younger kids to their sledding, and I followed him back to the house.

Chip stormed into the house, and I was right behind him. Daddy was nowhere in sight, but Mom was finally awake and at the kitchen sink. The slamming door got Mom's attention, and Chip started telling her what Daddy had been doing to me for years. She listened intently, and then Daddy entered the kitchen.

She looked at him, then at me and asked me if this was true. And I told her yes. She was visibly shaken by this but told me I was lying and told me to go to my room. Daddy was standing there with his mouth open, obviously shocked that the truth was out. Chip started yelling at them both. He was hysterical, and as I ran up the stairs, I heard him swinging and clawing at Daddy.

I was in my room and heard the screaming and yelling, and I was scared for Chip's life and my own. I had no idea what Daddy was going to do to me. Chip and Daddy were still physically fighting each other, and my mom was yelling at them both to stop. Finally, Daddy gave up and stormed out of the house, slamming the door behind him.

After a few minutes, when it was quiet, I eased open my bedroom door and looked down the hall, and there was Chip lying at the foot of the stairs, on the floor, crying with blood all over his face. And my heart was absolutely full of fear. I didn't know where Mom was, but besides Chips whimpering, it was quiet, and the tension was higher than I had ever felt in my life. I was scared to go downstairs, so I quietly closed my door and lay down on my bed, crying and scared.

Finally, I heard Chip down in his room through the heater duct, and I snuck out of my room and quietly moved down the hall and down the few stairs to the living room. I didn't see Mom and assumed she was up in her bedroom. I went downstairs to the basement to Chip's room and saw him sitting on his bed, and my heart hurt for him. His eyes were almost swollen shut, and there were cuts on his face. He was sitting there with his head in his hands, crying. I went over and sat down next to him and told him I was scared. He lifted one arm and put it over my shoulder and said, "Me too."

I tried to explain to him I was so glad he confronted Mom and Daddy but was so sorry he got beat up again. I told him I didn't know what to do, and he told me he didn't either. We sat on his bed, and we cried together. We were both scared of Daddy. He was terrible to both of us. My poor brother had been in so many fistfights with him in the past few years. I remembered my mom always crying and screaming to break them up. Daddy had caught Chip smoking in the basement once, and he took the cigarette from him and put it out by rubbing the burning end into my brother's cheek.

Daddy was gone to a motel, and every night Mom went to see him. I remember all four of us kids sitting on the big blue couch in the living room, watching television while she was gone. We watched a lot of the shows as a family, but tonight, it was just us kids. And we were all on edge. We sat alone and quiet, not knowing what would happen next. Pam and Steve were too young to understand. Chip and I dreaded the unknown. Would Daddy come back home, or would he be gone forever? We felt like it was our fault the family was broken up, and we felt the weight of it all. But we wished with all of our hearts that Daddy was gone for good. Mom came home from the motel and told all four of us, "Your daddy is coming home this weekend."

Chip stood up and said defiantly, "If he comes home, I'm leaving."

And Mom replied, "Then leave because he is coming home."

The rest of us just sat on the couch, looking at Mom like we couldn't believe what she was saying. I wanted to shout out and beg Mom not to let Daddy come home, but I knew she was not on our side and would not listen. The next day, Daddy came home, and Chip packed up a small bag and left without a word. The next time I saw him was years later, when we lived in Charleston, South Carolina.

Life was different from then on, mainly because Chip wasn't there, and I felt all alone. Daddy didn't sneak into my room anymore. But now that Chip was gone, Daddy started beating me instead. It was as if he wanted to punish me for telling on him, and he found any reason to turn his belt on me. He would take it off and fold it in half, but he held the two ends in his hand and hit me with the belt buckle. I dreaded the beatings in a different way. They seemed worse than the midnight visits to my bed. Daddy beat me for any reason—if I answered the phone wrong, if I looked at him wrong, if I wasn't in my room studying when he came home, if the dishes weren't done. Sometimes even if I spoke, he beat me. He found a reason almost every day to whip me with that belt, and as he swung the belt, he would yell at me and tell me how stupid and ugly I was and called me a whore. I remember feeling very hopeless once Chip left. I was all alone, Pam and Steve were too young, and Mom didn't care. She had started spending her time up in the bedroom, drinking, and us kids were alone.

Music came to my rescue again, and this time, it was the Beatles, whom I love to this day. Mom must have let me buy some albums because I didn't have any money, but I had two of their first albums: *Meet the Beatles* and *Please, Please Me*. Oh, I loved the Beatles, and I knew every word to every song. I played their albums over and over and couldn't get enough. We watched them on the *Ed Sullivan Show*, and I remember my heart melting and Daddy making fun of their long hair. Everyone seemed to love Paul McCartney best. But Ringo Starr was not the cutest one, just like me, so he was my favorite.

I loved Ringo so much that when we bought a parakeet, I named him Ringo. One day, Ringo fell into his water bowl. He was probably already dead, but I called Mom at work and asked her what should I do. She told me she didn't know but that I should try to keep him warm and dry. He was cold and wet, so I wrapped his limp body in a washcloth and carefully put him in the oven and turned it on. I watched him through the window, and he never made a move. I finally took him out and his limp head told me he was dead. I had a Ringo model kit that came in a box (the kind of models you used to glue together), and I buried Ringo in the backyard in the Ringo box.

Quitting School

I was in eighth grade, and one day, my homeroom teacher saw fresh but all-too-familiar welts and bruising on my legs. And I could see the hurt look on her face again. This day, she came up to my desk and told me to follow her out of the classroom. As we walked, she told me she was taking me to the counselor's office, and I wondered if I was in trouble. What had Daddy done to me now?

We walked into the windowed room, and I sat down on a chair, looking down to the floor. My teacher sat next to me and began to tell the counselor how many times she had seen me come to school with evidence of being beaten. The counselor asked me who was beating me, and I looked up at her and didn't know where to start. I said nothing. There was a whole life I could tell her, and I figured it would only open a bigger can of worms that she was not prepared for, so I didn't say a thing. Besides, Mom wouldn't believe me, so why would they believe me? The counselor told me all I had to do was say who it was, and they would assist me in getting help. I knew if I told anyone about what Daddy was doing to me, they would tell the authorities, who would press charges, and it would be my word against his. Daddy was very smart and always got his way and did what he wanted to do. I knew with all my heart he could convince them that I deserved it, and they would let him go. And then he would turn on me. I always lived in fear that he would kill me, so I again told my counselor I couldn't tell them. They tried to get me to talk, and I just couldn't. I knew it was something I could not win—not against Daddy.

I went home from school and never got another chance to tell them because I never went back. I knew what Daddy was doing to me wasn't right, but I knew I would never win. I lost hope that anything would ever change, so I started running away from home.

Daddy had a friend named Doris, who was a single lady who had two daughters, and I thought they were family of some sort because that is what Daddy told us. Her two daughters were Sandy and Sheila, and we became friends. I spent a lot of time at their house, spending the night in their extra bedroom. I went to their house to spend the night one day and just stayed. This was my first official "runaway." Daddy didn't know I was there, and I wondered what he thought when I didn't come home. I was deathly afraid he would find out I was there and that I had not gone to school.

One day, Sandy and Sheila had some of their friends over when their mom wasn't home, and they started drinking cherry sloe gin and convinced me to drink some too. It wasn't long before I was lying on the couch, and my head was swimming. I was so dizzy it made me sick, and I threw up all over the white carpet. And it wasn't a pretty sight. They were angry at me, and they worked to get it cleaned up. But it wasn't coming clean, so they put a rug over the stain. I passed out on the couch. This was the first time I drank alcohol, and it made me deathly ill.

Doris came home and saw all of us drunk and saw the purple stain on her white shag carpet and ordered all of us out of the house. Sandy and Sheila were driving me back to my house, and Daddy happened to be home. When he saw us pull into the driveway, he immediately came running out of the house, waving a gun. I yelled for the girls to back up and go fast. The girls saw Daddy with the gun, and it put a scare into them. We backed up quickly and started to go down the street when a bullet came through the back window. The girls screamed, and I got on the floor in the back seat, and we drove as fast as we could back to their house.

We all ran into the house and told their mother, Doris, what Daddy had done. Doris got mad at me and told me to get out and said it was all my fault that her daughters were almost killed. That night, they took me back to my house, and with nowhere else to go, I snuck into my bedroom through my window and got into my bed. I hoped he had not heard me because if he found out I was home, I knew he would beat me, possibly kill me, if he found out I was there, so I slept all night. And before he found me, I climbed out my bedroom window and went to my friend Gloria's house.

Her mother, being a bit drifty, didn't seem to mind or notice I was there. Things seemed a little more permanent for me at Gloria's, so one day, I snuck back into my house during the day when Daddy was at work and Mom was asleep. I packed a bag of clothes, all my albums (about ten), and a garnet birthstone ring Mom had given me for my thirteenth birthday.

It had been almost a month, and I almost felt like I had been adopted by Gloria's family. No one seemed to mind I was there all the time. It all changed one day when Gloria got in trouble, and I had to leave. A week or so before I had to leave, Gloria asked if she could wear my garnet ring, and I let her. Later on, I asked for it back, and she said she wanted to wear it for a while longer. And then abruptly, I had to leave and ended up leaving with her still wearing my ring, and I had to leave all my albums too.

With nowhere to go, I ended up back home. And of course, Daddy beat me with that wicked belt buckle, yelling his cruel words—"Stupid, ugly, whore."

After that day, I tried to stay in my room; but one day, Daddy called me into the living room and had me sit down on the couch. He told me that Mom had a little pistol and that it was missing. He said he believed I had taken it, which I hadn't. He pulled out a small contraption he called a lie detector test and slid the clips onto my fingers: one clip on the pointer and one on the ring finger of my right hand. He told me if I told the truth, I would be okay; but if I lied, he was going to send me to a reform school.

He divided the house in half and asked if the gun was upstairs or downstairs. I had to say no to every question, and this would tell him if I was lying or not. And only he could read the results to the test. He continued dividing the house in half, all the way down to the basement. The basement was unfinished except Chip's empty bedroom and a very large shipping box where blankets, sheets, and towels were stored. He again asked if it was on the left side or the right side of the room. Saying the obligatory *no* to each, he narrowed it down to the item on the left—the large shipping box. He opened the lid, picked up a blanket, and sure enough, underneath was the gun. When he picked up the gun, I was truly afraid he was going to shoot me, but he didn't. Instead, he picked it up and then looked at me and said, "You stole the gun and put it in here, didn't you?" I looked at him and wondered how he had done that, and fearfully, I told him no, I hadn't. But he grabbed my arm and dragged me upstairs to my room and got his belt out and began beating me, yelling the whole time, "You are so stupid, you ugly little whore." He was almost fanatical, and I thought he had gone crazy. I knew I hadn't even seen or touched the gun, but he made me out to be a liar. And now he was beating me for lying.

It didn't make sense, but I knew he had manipulated the entire process to send me to a reform school. I was hurting and exhausted by his punishment, and I lay on the bed out of breath from sobbing and feeling totally defeated. I didn't understand why Daddy hated me so much. It was like he wanted me to be in trouble so he could beat me. And when I wasn't in trouble, he created a situation so I would be "in trouble" just so he could beat me. He had succeeded in breaking my spirit, and I just gave up trying.

One day, Daddy came into my bedroom while I was sleeping, and he jerked the covers off me, then yelled at me, "Get up, you stupid whore." He told me to put some clothes on and come downstairs, and I knew something was getting ready to happen.

When I was dressed, I went downstairs apprehensively. He was waiting for me and got up and grabbed my arm and took me out to the car. We drove in silence. I had no idea where we were going and was afraid to ask. He pulled up in front of the local police station and said to me, "Come on." I got out of the car, scared to death, and he took me by the arm. We walked up the three stories of stairs to a police officer, sitting behind a desk.

We went up to his desk and sat down in the two chairs in front of the desk, and Daddy proceeded to tell the officer, "She is a runaway, and I can't control her. I want her locked up."

The officer looked at me a little shocked and looked at my dad and said, "What do you want me to do with her?"

Daddy started telling him about all the times I had run away and that I had quit school, and right in the middle of his "speech," I asked if I could go to the bathroom.

It was an older building, and the bathroom had high ceilings with bare wood walls and a big window next to the toilet. I pulled my shorts down and sat down on the toilet, and the breeze coming in cooled my face. That's when I realized I had an open window with no screen on it right next to me.

My mind raced. Could I possibly escape from this police station? When I finished, I looked out the window and saw the awning over the window below me just like the one above me and thought to myself, *I can jump on that awning, and it might hold me. Then I can jump to the roof of the building next to it.* I was in a three-story building, and I was scared of heights. But I knew this was my chance, and I had to jump. *What if the awning doesn't hold me? What if the police put out a search for me?* But I quickly realized it was jump or go to jail, so I jumped.

The building next to us was three stories too, but the back half was only two stories. I jumped down to the awning of the second-story window, and it held me, then jumped across to the roof of the other building. As I ran across the roof, I looked left and noticed a wall full of big picture windows facing me, and inside those windows were policemen all sitting at tables eating. It was like a lunchroom for the police! My heart jumped, and I just scampered as fast as I could across the roof. I looked over the edge of the building and saw a police car in the alley, and without hesitation, I jumped from the second story onto the roof of the police car then in two steps jumped down to the hood and to the ground, and I never looked back.

I was out on the street and started running as fast as I could down the sidewalk in the opposite direction of the police station. I was almost out of breath when a car traveling in the same direction down the street slowed down, and the man in the car leaned over and rolled down his passenger window and said, "Hey, what's going on? Do you need a ride?"

I was huffing and puffing and told him, "My dad is trying to put me in jail. I just jumped out of the window of the police station."

"Whoa," he said. "Get in the car. I'll take care of you." I got into his car.

We traveled the rest of the way down the street to a large four-floor apartment building at the end of the street. The man pulled into a parking place on the street and said, "Hey, I have to run up and get something out of my apartment. Do you want to go with me?"

I felt like he had saved me, and I felt safe, so I said yes.

We walked up the stairs together to the door at the top of the stairs on the second floor. He used a key to open the door, and we walked into a studio-type apartment. I walked across the room and sat down on his couch, and I could see the whole apartment from where I sat. I scanned the room. There was a fireplace with a mantle above it to my left. The front door was right in front of me, and to its right was the door to a bathroom. And to the right of that was an open kitchen that was part of the bedroom that was to my immediate right. It was all one big room with the bathroom as the only room enclosed.

As I sat on the couch, I watched him take the key, lock the door, then he walked over to the fireplace and dropped the key into a German beer stein on the mantle—above my reach. And I wondered if that was just habit or if I should be worried.

I sat on the couch, waiting for him, my heart thumping in my chest, wondering what the heck he was doing, and watched as he went into the bathroom and turned on the water in the bathtub. That's when I froze, and I held my breath. And I knew—I should be worried. Not sure what to do, fear overtook me; and as I stared at him, he came over to me and, in one big swoop, picked me up and threw me onto the bed and then threw himself on top of me. I started to struggle and told him to leave me alone. My arms were thrashing around, trying to hit his face, and it was then that I noticed I had scratched his face. It was bleeding. For some reason, the blood on his face made me think he was going to kill me if he realized he was bleeding, so I started really kicking and screaming. I was using my fists to try to hit him in the face and using my knees to kick at him and push him off me. He finally let loose of me in disgust and said, "All right, all right! Get out of here!" He stormed over to the beer stein on the mantle and took the key out, stomped over to the door, unlocked it, threw the door open, and ordered me to get out. I ran out of there, down the stairs, and onto the sidewalk of the street as fast as I could and started to run.

I ran as fast as I could for about ten minutes until my lungs were burning, my side was hurting, and I couldn't catch my breath. I slowed down next to a park that was full of benches and picnic tables. I went inside the park, away from the road, and sat down on one of the park benches, out of breath from running. Once I caught my breath and calmed down a little, I started crying. *Why was all this happening to me? Why?* I screamed in my head. I didn't understand any of it, and my mind was racing trying to understand. My fierce will broke into pieces and fell to the ground in front of me in the form of tears. I gave up; I surrendered. I was thirteen years old and felt like I was ninety.

I walked home, feeling sick, empty, defeated, and I had nowhere else to go. Instead of sneaking in my bedroom window, I walked right into the front door of the house, and not even looking at the "family" sitting on the couch, I went up to my bedroom. I was exhausted and felt like I just didn't care anymore. Lock me up, kill me, put me away in a reform school, I didn't care. I hated myself, my life, Mom, Daddy, everything. I hated it all.

It was evident I was broken, and it was almost like they sensed that and laid off me for a while. Daddy stopped beating me for about a month, and it was almost peaceful. I should have known better. It was just the calm before the storm.

One morning, my dad came into my room and jerked off the covers while I was sleeping, as he liked to do, and he yelled at me, "Get up and get dressed."

I got up, got dressed, and went downstairs. Daddy was sitting on the couch alone. No one else was around. He said, "Let's go." And without another word, I followed him out to the big blue Ford. We drove for a while and ended up on the outskirts of town. We pulled up in front of a brick building that had no windows, and the sign outside said "Salt Lake Valley Detention Center." I knew he was finally putting me in reform school.

We got out of the car and walked up the sidewalk side by side. He opened the glass door, and we went inside. He went to the front desk, and I stood behind him as he checked me in. And then he turned and left without saying a word. I didn't know what was going to happen next. I was scared to death, but I really didn't care. Nothing could be as bad as what I had already lived through, and I didn't feel like I had a family anymore. The uniformed woman took me back through a security door that opened to a room full of long metal picnic-type tables. The big kitchen area was to my right as we walked through, and then we entered a hallway that was full of closed doors. Each door had a tiny window in it, and as I walked down the hall, I could see faces looking at me. She delivered me to another woman who took over, and she asked me my name and then shuffled some papers, made some notes, and then told me to follow her. She took me down the hallway, past the windowed doors, and opened a door on the right and told me to go inside. I went in and stood in the middle of the small room, and she followed me. She put some baby-blue clothes, a white towel and washcloth, soap, shampoo, toothbrush, and toothpaste on the bed and told me to change into the clothes. I was embarrassed I had to dress down to my panties, and the only bra I had was filthy. And I didn't have enough to fill the cups, so I was embarrassed about that too. I was skinny and scrawny. I put on the blue "prison clothes," and she told me the rules as I dressed. We would be let out for meals and an outdoor time. We could shower every day, and we could use the curlers they had. But they counted the bobby pins, so I was to make sure not to lose a bobby pin, and that was it for the rules.

The walls to my new room were solid concrete, and there was a concrete slab for a bed with a mattress on it. It did have sheets on it. There was a stainless steel toilet and sink next to the bed, but there was no chair or table, just the bed to sit on. Without a word, she left the room, locked the door, and I heard her walking away. This was it—I was actually in the reform school my dad told me he would put me in. I wondered how long I had to live there. I figured until I was eighteen, a little more than four more years.

I lay down on the bed and took the first peaceful nap I had taken in a very long time. I slept like a baby until they woke me up and said it was time for dinner. I went into the room with the tables, and there were girls my age everywhere sitting at the tables eating or standing in line getting their food. There were girls who teased me, and girls who were friendly and kind. The uniformed women kept a watch on all of us, but they weren't mean. It was soon known I was not one of the bad girls. I was accepted by some of the quieter girls and cared for by the women. I showered every day and used the curlers every night, and the next day I took out the curlers and counted the bobby pins.

After a couple of weeks there, they gave me a job in the kitchen. My job was to make toast out of a couple loaves of bread and put grape jelly on half and strawberry jam on the other half. I began to feel worthy enough to live and felt like I had purpose. I actually enjoyed the girls I had made friends with, and I listened to their stories, and they heard mine. They felt sorry for me and I for them, but talking to them and hearing their stories made me realize I wasn't alone in my misery. They felt like sisters of the same father, and I appreciated them so very much. The women in the uniforms were also kind. My life was peaceful and had boundaries, but I was actually enjoying being in the reform school (I later found out it was a detention center). It was safe, and I was not afraid. I slept like a baby every night, and I didn't mind at all being "behind bars." I found a new family, and it was feeling good.

Then everything changed. I had been there for a few months when one day my dad walked in, and he was ready to take me home. I went to my cell room, and one of the women helped me change clothes. I cried and told her I was afraid to go home and didn't want to go. She told me she understood, but I had to go, and there was nothing she could do. She told me if Daddy did anything else, I should tell someone and get help. And I agreed that I would. I had to quickly say my goodbyes to the women caring for us and the friends I had made. Daddy took me out the front doors to the outside, and I got in the big blue car that was there in front waiting. I was heartbroken to have to leave. We didn't go back to our house in Murray,

Utah. Instead, we drove all the way to South Carolina. Daddy must have just left me long enough to get the house sold and packed up. We ended up at a rented house on White Drive in Charleston, South Carolina.

Charleston, South Carolina (1964–1969)

It was an awkward three days traveling across the country. At first, Steve and Pam didn't know what to say to me, but I could tell they were happy to have me back in the fold as they smiled sheepishly at me. My parents were quiet but acted like I had never been gone, and we all got back to normal pretty quickly. We slept in motel rooms with two beds: us three kids in one bed, and Mom and Daddy in another. And we kids played road games all the way.

Mom put me into eighth grade in Charleston. I felt totally out of place because I was a runaway and had spent the last few months in a reform school. I was too skinny and tall and had messy, unmanageable hair. Mom picked out and bought our clothes at Sears and Roebuck, and they were not the fashionable ones at all. Because I was about a foot taller than anyone and had big feet, I felt like I stuck out like a sore thumb and got attention I didn't want to have. I was a loner and wanted to be, and I didn't trust anyone.

I did try to be friends with a black girl named Debbie because I felt sorry for her, and she seemed to be alone like I was. I confronted her, and she questioned why I would want to have anything to do with her. I told her I didn't have any friends and she didn't either, so she accepted my offer. And we were friends for about two months, but we always got harassed.

Then three girls at school befriended me one day, and I thought they were sincere. I recognized them as girls I had seen at school, but I didn't know them. After school one day, they came to my house in a car, and all three came to the door, and one of them asked if I wanted to go for a ride in their car. I thought, *Wow, how fun to hang around with friends*; and since I was home alone, I thought, *Why not?* and readily went with them.

We only went to the end of the street where there was an elementary school, and we drove up to the side of the building. We all got out of the car, and as I wondered why we were there, one of the girls behind me pushed me. I tripped and fell to the ground. The other two girls started hitting me with their fists, and then one girl climbed onto my belly. She had a big plastic ball ring on her right hand, and she slammed it into my face. She kept slamming until I was begging her to stop. She finally stopped, and they all stood above me and took turns spitting down on me; then they got into their car and left me lying there on the grass, crying.

I sat up, wiping their spit off my face and spitting out my own blood. My whole face hurt. Smoothing down my hair, I sat there dazed and hurting and wondered why these girls would do this to me. It just didn't make sense to me. Today I believe it was because I had befriended Debbie, the black girl. I finally got up and slowly walked home. I wasn't sure if I should tell my parents what had happened to my face. I figured they probably would not care that I got beat up. My dad would find a way to blame the whole thing on me, so I stayed away from everyone as much as I could, making excuses so I could just stay in my room.

What I realized is that people don't know how to handle people who are different than them. In 1964 and 1965, when I was thirteen/fourteen, the South was turbulent, and whites didn't mix with blacks. It was taboo to befriend a black girl. I guess they thought they were teaching me a lesson.

Most of the girls I went to school with had the cutest clothes and perfect hair. They had friends that looked like them, and I was always the different one. I was about a foot taller than anyone else and was always awkward and uncoordinated. I had big feet, no boobs, and looked quite like a stick with no curves and unruly long curly blonde hair that I never could get right. I was the one that gave them the creeps, so they avoided me. Add to that the fact I had been sexually and physically abused for so long, which also affected who I was and how I looked. I was withdrawn and didn't know how to stand up for myself, so they picked on me and bullied me to no end. And my dad felt he could abuse and bully me too because I was stupid and ugly, and none of them found value in me.

We moved from our little house on White Drive in Charleston to the Isle of Palms, which was just over the Ashley Cooper River. It was 1965, and I turned fourteen without much fanfare. I felt like an ugly, stupid, awkward, unwanted, and damaged nobody, and nothing was good at home anymore. Mom and Daddy were drinking and spending their evenings in the bedroom while Steve, Pam, and I made our own dinner. It was usually a pot of grits we made almost every day after school, and we sat around the table eating it with melted butter and salt. Sometimes this was our only meal besides the lunch at school.

I guess Daddy thought I had changed my ways by going to the detention home, and he didn't beat me or sneak into my bedroom at night anymore. He and Mom's drinking had moved to a new level, and they both pretty much ignored us, for which I was thankful. But I didn't take any of that for granted. I didn't trust him. I didn't go back to school, and they didn't make me.

Instead, I got up and went to the beach most days while my younger brother and sister went to school. I loved the breezy, sunny days on the beautiful beaches there in Isle of Palms. The distance to the beach was easy to get to on my bike, and I remember going to the end of the island and finding thousands of sand dollars in the shallower parts of the water. I wished I could just live there forever and never go home.

Then one day I decided to do it, to live on the beach forever, but I had to go to a beach where they wouldn't find me. I decided on Folly Beach in Charleston. Mom and Daddy probably wouldn't even notice I was gone because they spent their days in the bedroom, and we barely saw them anymore.

Daddy had a silver dollar collection that was in a velvet Crown Royal bag, and though it was stealing, and the bag was heavy, I took it from the house and put it in my bicycle basket. I gathered up some of my clothes and put them in a bag. I had a friend who lived in my neighborhood there in Isle of Palms. I rode my bike to her house to say goodbye. I told her I was running away for good and was going to get a job at Folly Beach at the arcade. She listened and understood, and she gave me a little blue suitcase for my clothes and a little blanket and some toiletries. I told her thank you and hugged her goodbye, and I rode my bike most of the day across the bridges all the way to Folly Beach.

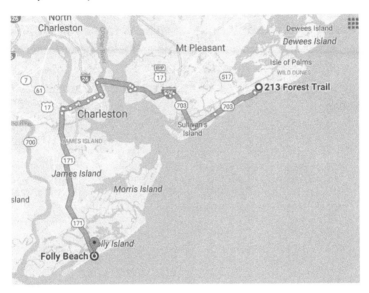

When I got to Folly Beach, I took a right on the beach and down the beach a way. I found a weathered, abandoned house I thought I would check out. It was on stilts, and there were no stairs. It was a bit difficult to get into, but I was a tree climber and climbed up the cross boards into the house. The house was in pretty dangerous shape. It had holes in the floor, and there were no doors or windows. But it looked like perfect shelter for me, so I made it my temporary home. I found a room in the back and put down my suitcase, then climbed back down and left the beach, walking up the road to find something to eat. I was thirsty and hungry and found a little outdoor burger place and went up to the window to ask for a cheeseburger, fries, and a Pepsi. They looked at me strange when I handed them the silver dollar, but after a brief shock, they took it. I wolfed down the cheeseburger and fries and was stuffed. It was early evening by the time I was done, so I made my way back to the empty house, climbed back in, and went to sleep using my little blanket as a pillow. Listening to the waves of the ocean put me to sleep, and I slept like a baby all night long.

I hung around the beach for a couple of weeks and ate at the cheeseburger place once a day. Finally, one morning I ventured away from Folly Beach and rode my bicycle into Charleston, and that's when I came across the Biff Burger. I went up to the window to order a cheeseburger and a Pepsi and noticed a "Help Wanted" sign in the window. When the girl gave me my order, I asked her about the sign. And she told me I had to talk to the manager. The manager's name was Wendy.

Wendy—Manager of Biff Burger

Wendy was tall and had short brown hair and dark-brown eyes, and she was so nice to me I couldn't believe it. We sat at the picnic table out front and talked about who I was and where I came from. I only told her a little about my past. I didn't tell her I was a runaway. She treated me with respect, and though I was not sure whether to trust her or not, I felt like she was kind and understanding. She asked me if I had ever worked, and I told her I hadn't. Then she asked me if I could cut hot dogs, and I told her I sure could. Then she told me to come back the next day, and I could start working for her there at the Biff Burger.

I made my way back to Folly Beach so happy I couldn't believe it! My first job ever. I was elated! I couldn't believe I had gotten a job and was going to make my own money! I made my way back to the beach on my bike. I decided I would grab my little blanket and go play on the beach next to that beautiful ocean to celebrate, and when I climbed up to the entry and into my "room," I found my little blue suitcase filled with my clothes was gone! I couldn't believe it, and it actually scared me. Who would climb up there and steal my little suitcase? I was heartbroken and now was a little frightened to stay there since someone knew I was there, but it didn't stop me from going down to my beloved beach, and I celebrated my new job.

At least I still had my blanket and the bag of silver dollars, so I climbed down out of the house and laid my blanket on the beach and dug a little hole in the sand and put the small bag of silver dollars under the blanket. Then I went down to the water's edge and sat down where the waves were lapping at the shore and my legs. I stared out at the ocean, daydreaming about a day when I could be grown up, and everything would be over. And at that moment, I felt pretty free, and that was good. I wasn't even scared that Daddy would ever find me.

I lay back onto the warm sand and looked up at the white clouds and talked to God. I told him I wasn't sure where he lived up there but just wanted to say thank you for the job and wondered if he could help me a little bit more. I told him I was alone, sleeping in that broken-down house on the beach and that someone had stolen all my clothes. He didn't say anything, and before I knew it, I was waking up, sunk into the sand, water lapping at my butt and covered with sand that the ocean had deposited onto me. I got up and walked deeper into the warm water and sat down and got wet all the way up to my neck. I dunked my head under water and swirled my head around to wash my hair. I rubbed my arms and legs with sand and got out feeling clean. I got out of the water and went over to the outside public shower and rinsed off the salty water, then headed back to my blanket to dry.

When I was somewhat dry, I got a little hungry, and I was walking up Folly Beach Road (the road that leads to Folly Beach), feeling clean and a combination of hungry, happy for my new job, and lonely. I was walking along, kicking a rock up the sidewalk when I happened to look up. Straight ahead of me was Daddy, and he was running full force toward me. I saw Mom, Pam, and Steve walking behind him. And I turned around and ran as fast as I could run. I could hear Daddy behind me yelling, "Patricia! Patricia!" (He never called me Patsy.) I ignored him and turned left onto the street that ran beside a restaurant and ran for my life. I was a good runner at school; sometimes my legs ran faster than my body. My legs were long, and they got me going fast, so I easily outran him.

He must have gotten tired because when I looked back, he was not there. I kept running for a while because though he may not have been as fast as me, I knew he could easily trick me. I got to a place in an alley where I could hide. I crouched next to a fence behind a trash can and stayed there quietly for a few minutes. I watched to see if he would come around the corner, and he didn't show. I didn't want to walk back to my "house" because I figured that beach was where they were going, so I got down on the beach and walked in the other direction. I hung around the other end of the beach for a couple of hours until I figured they should be gone; then I made my way back to my "house" and didn't see them anywhere.

Thankfully, my bicycle was still there, leaning against the wooden pylons of the house. I put my blanket and the bag of money into the basket, which was on the front of the bike and walked it to Folly Beach Road, where I got on and started to ride. I found a secondhand store a few streets back and went in to see what they had. I found a couple pair of shorts and shirts and even a bathing suit, and all of it only cost me about two or three of the silver dollars. I went back to the hamburger place and ordered a cheeseburger and a Pepsi. I sat at one of the outside tables and ate the delicious meal; it had lettuce, tomatoes, and mayonnaise on it. I felt like I was getting a good meal.

I made my way back to the house and sat cross-legged, looking out at the ocean from the window. Thankful I was not caught by my dad, I wondered why he was chasing me and calling to me. I had been gone for a couple of weeks or so, and it was actually surprising to see them all at Folly Beach. I thought about the last few years at home and wondered again why my life had been so difficult. My heart was heavy, and I felt overwhelmed with sorrow and started to cry. I was grateful to be away from that house and my parents, but I also felt like I had survived a war, and I was so tired and wounded.

Staring out at the ocean, I began to think of my younger days when we used to play on the beach in Gulf Breeze, Florida. I could almost see Chip and I crouched over the sand, looking for shells— my long white blonde hair a mess hanging in my face and my favorite pink bathing suit hugging my body. I closed my eyes and watched in my memory and listened to the gentle lapping of the waves coming into shore and a few seagulls squawking in the distance. Life was so simple back then. I was so young and innocent, and life was easy and so carefree. My heart yearned for those days.

Then I realized the reality of the moment, and that was that Daddy had not caught me. And he didn't know where I was. I had a job, and I was feeling like I might really make it. Staring out at the ocean, I daydreamed until the sun went down, and it was time to go to sleep. I used the bag of my new clothes as a pillow and slept like a baby all night long.

The next morning, everything went with me to Biff Burger (my bag of clothes, the little blanket, and the silver dollars). It took me over an hour to ride my bicycle to my new job. Wendy met me by the back door and told me where I could park my bike. She had me fill out some papers, and I left some of the spots blank—like my birthdate, which would show I was only fourteen years old. She looked over the papers and didn't have any questions; then she took me up to the front and introduced me to everyone who was there. She took me into a side room and showed me how to cut the hot dogs on this special wooden cutting board. There were grooves cut into the board where you laid the hot dog and only half of the hot-dog showed. Cutting slices into the half of the hot dog made the hot dogs curl into a circle when they were cooked, and then they were put into some BBQ sauce to soak. Then it would go on a hamburger bun. Biff Burger was famous for their BBQ sauce, and we sold a lot of those hot dogs.

I worked every day that week and got my first paycheck, and though I don't remember how much it was, it was a lot to me! There was a department store across the street, and I went in to cash my check. But they asked for ID. I didn't have any, so I went back to the Biff Burger and asked Wendy if she could cash my paycheck. She did, and before I left on my bicycle, she let me have a cheeseburger and fries, which I gobbled up.

Mr. Margiotta's Drugstore

I rode my bike to work every day, and one day on my way "home" to the abandoned house, I noticed an "Apartment for Rent" sign in Mr. Margiotta's drugstore. I went inside and asked Mr. Margiotta how much he wanted for the apartment. After his shocked look at me, he said in his very Italian accent, "I have a home for you. It's only fifty dollars a month."

We went out the back door of the drugstore and went up a flight of stairs to a landing and a door that he opened with a key, and we walked in. It opened into the living room, and I was happy to see it was totally furnished. A hallway from the living room went back to a kitchen on the left and a bathroom on the right; then at the end of the hallway, it opened to a big room that was a combination bedroom/dining room. The bed was tucked into a little cove in the wall, and it was all very charming. There was a dining table and chairs near the kitchen. "I love it!" I told him, and I asked him if I could move in next week when I got my check.

He gave me a smile and gave me the key and said, "That's okay. You stay here now." My face and my heart smiled by his kindness.

I took the key, told him thank-you, and went outside to get my bicycle and brought it around to the back. I took my little bag of clothes and silver dollars up the stairs, went inside my "new apartment," and sat down on the couch. Wow, I had a job, and now I had an apartment. I was so happy, and I felt so grown-up!

The apartment was much closer to Biff Burger as well, so I didn't have to ride my bicycle for an hour to get there. I was amazed and so happy about my good luck and so happy to be away from Daddy and from Mom, who hadn't been a mother to me in a very long time.

I wondered if Wendy and Mr. Margiotta were angels sent to take care of me.

I continued to work at Biff Burger and live above Mr. Margiotta's drugstore, and though I was alone, I loved it. I felt safe and continued to relish my sleep. I knew Daddy would not wake me up in the middle of the night ever again.

Mr. Margiotta had a soda fountain in his drugstore, and sometimes when I didn't eat at Biff Burger for free, I would eat at the soda fountain. I didn't know how to cook anything but grits, so if I ate at home, that was what I had, except a sandwich now and then.

One day, I went to make a sandwich; and when I opened the drawer to get the bread, a mouse had gotten into the loaf and ate a good chunk of it. It had also gotten into my banana-flavored "weight-on" pills I had found in Mr. Margiotta's drugstore.

I knew I had to get rid of the mouse, so I bought a mousetrap and set it up, which took forever to do, and put it in the drawer. It didn't take long. Later that evening, I heard a *snap*; and sure enough, I caught the mouse.

Now came the dilemma. For some reason, the trap didn't kill him instantly, and he was still alive and struggling to get free. I really did not know what to do. I just couldn't work up the guts to open the trap and let him loose, and the only other alternative was to let him eventually die in the trap. I felt so bad for him and really did not like the whole situation, so I decided to bury him. I found an old shoebox and opened it up, and it seemed so big for the small mouse. So I put a washcloth in it and fluffed it up a little. It didn't help that much, but it seemed more comfortable for his coffin than the big plain cardboard box. I picked up the mousetrap using a knife and put the entire trap and mouse into the box and put the lid on. I felt so terrible because I could still hear him struggling to get free. Not having any other options, I took the box downstairs, and there in the back lot, I dug a hole in the sand with a big spoon big enough for the shoebox and then placed it inside the grave and covered it up. "I'm sorry, Mr. Mouse," I said as a prayer. His little carcass is probably still in that box, buried behind Mr. Margiotta's drugstore.

Another adventure I had in Mr. Margiotta's apartment: there was a large brown floor furnace in the living room that ran by propane. It can get chilly in Charleston in the winter because of the humidity, and this was one of those days. I got on the floor to figure out how to turn it on. Somehow I figured out how to get the gas going, and then I realized it had to be lit. I didn't have any matches, so I went into the kitchen to get matches and got back down on the floor. It took a couple of times on the striker to light, but the instant it lit, the flame of the match set the gas in the air on fire. A huge blast burned the right-hand side of my face, my eyebrow, and eyelashes. I screamed and jumped back. The blast hurt and scared me, but I got it lit and learned a big lesson about gas.

One day, I was coming home from Biff Burger, and there in front of the drugstore were a couple of kids, and they had a big box of puppies! I stopped my bike and went over to the little black babies. I picked one up and smelled its puppy breath and felt its soft fur on the little body. One of them had white paws and a little white patch on his forehead, and my heart just had to have him. I ran inside and asked Mr. Margiotta if I could have a puppy in the apartment, and he said I could (all the floors were wood). I went back and asked if I could have the one with the white paws. The little girl picked him up and handed him to me, and I immediately named him Boots.

Boots slept with me at night and lived in a box during the day when I was gone. Once he was potty-trained, he got the run of the apartment. One day, I came home from work, and he had chewed up all the pillows on the couch and the pillows from my bed! There was white filler everywhere in the living room. It almost filled the room. I was shocked when I opened the door to see the cloud of filling. I laughed, and he played in it while I cleaned it up.

The next thing he found were my shoes. Now, I didn't have that many, but what I did have, he had taken into the living room. And one by one, he chewed them completely apart.

I spent my fifteenth birthday with Boots because I didn't have any human friends, and it was okay because I didn't feel like I needed any. I actually liked being a loner and taking care of myself. Being without Daddy was a new experience, and that was a wonderful thing. I guess it was worth it to spend my birthdays alone.

To occupy myself, I started writing out prayers to God. Prayers that said, "Thank you for taking care of me." "Thank you for this house." "Thank you for helping me get away from Daddy." I decorated them with my crayons and made pretty borders of green vines and different colored flowers. Then I would tape them on the wall above my bed. After a while, the wall was almost full of my prayers, and it was quite colorful.

I believed in God, and my prayers were always simple. The colorful flowered paper prayers were my offering to him, and I hoped that he could hear me. I always thought he lived on a cloud above us and that he watched over us from there, but somehow I knew I was communicating with him.

After I had been living in my apartment above the drugstore and working at Biff Burger for a few months, I got the guts to call my mom and dad at the house. I realized I was only fifteen, but I had a job and an apartment; and for some reason, I needed them to "approve" of me not coming home and that it was okay that I wasn't going to school. I made the call, and Mom answered the phone. She seemed uninterested that I was even calling.

I did most of the talking and told her about my job, my apartment, and my dog in hopes I could convince her I was established and could make it on my own. She listened quietly and finally, she said, "I don't care. Do what you want to do." It took me a minute to respond, but then I invited her and Daddy to dinner at my apartment. Lo and behold, she agreed to come.

As the day got closer, I got more nervous and almost scared because I did not know what to expect. It wasn't Mom I worried about; it was my dad who scared me the most. I didn't know if he would walk in and beat me, drag me home, or call the police once he knew where I lived. This was a huge risk I was taking, but I had to get their approval so I could cut the ties I had with them.

I tried to figure out what to do for the dinner. I did not have a clue how to cook anything, so it took me a while to put a whole dinner together. I finally bought a frozen turkey roll that I reheated in the oven, per the directions on the package. I made instant mashed potatoes with packaged gravy and canned peas. I set the table really pretty and folded napkins to go under the silverware.

They arrived at my apartment and knocked on the door, and I went to the door. With Boots by my side and my heart beating out of my chest, I opened it, and there they were, both my parents. Daddy didn't immediately grab me or do anything, and with my heart still beating wildly, I let them in to the living room. I walked down the hall and, just like Vanna White, showed them where the bathroom was to the right, the kitchen to the left; and then there we were in my huge bedroom, and to the left was the dining table all nicely set.

I turned around to see their response, and there was none. Their looks were blank, and it was like I was someone they didn't know. They were guests at a stranger's house.

There were no hugs or smiles—it was an inspection. Everything was matter of fact as they looked around. They sat down, and I went to the kitchen to get all the food and wondered what I was supposed to do to "break the ice."

They sat, not talking, and waited until I put the food on the table, and then they served themselves. It was pretty quiet, except small talk that I made about my job, my boss Wendy, Mr. Margiotta, Boots. I really had not talked to them one on one like this ever, and we were all very uncomfortable. Even Daddy, the man I feared the most, did not say much. I told them how I had gotten Boots, and they didn't ask me how I was doing or if I needed any money—nothing. They stayed to eat and then left. When they were gone, I sat down on the end of the bed and took a deep breath and started crying. Boots wandered up to me to figure out what was going on and helped me quit crying. I just sat there holding him and marveled that I was finally free of them. I had been released as their responsibility, and I was on my own. And it was such a relief. I didn't see my parents again for about three years.

Donald

Another birthday with Boots, I turned sixteen, and that was about when I met Donald in the drugstore downstairs. He was two years older than me, and he became a friend quickly. I guess he was really my very first boyfriend. He was very kind and took care of me like a Southern gentleman. He bought me ice cream at the drugstore fountain, and we walked hand in hand to McDonalds to get cheeseburgers. He was a bit awkward, and so was I since I had never had a boyfriend. After we had been seeing each other for a few months, he wanted me to meet his parents. He had a motorcycle that he rode, and he put me on the back of it and took me to his house on John's Island. His mom was sitting at her kitchen table, drinking buttermilk with corn bread mixed into it, and she had a big whole onion that she bit into like an apple. I sat there watching her eat, amazed. I had never seen anyone eat an onion like that before.

From Donald's house, we took a walk into the woods, and he held my hand as we walked. We sat under the big angel oak, and he told me how much he liked me and that he had joined the army and was going to Vietnam. He said he was going to be gone a whole year, and then he would be home, and he wanted me to wait for him. I knew what he was saying but did not fully understand what it meant to wait a whole year for him to return. All I knew was that he was my boyfriend, and I cared for him. I went to the airport with his family to say goodbye, and he went to boot camp. Before he left for Vietnam, he came home with a shaved head and a fancy diamond ring. He presented it to me before he left. It was a beautiful gold ring with diamonds in it, and I thought it was so romantic that he was giving me this ring. I accepted it and wore it. He gave me his overseas address, and I wrote him letters, and he wrote me back. There was about a month delay on delivery, but at least we got each other's letters. He sent me stories about what they were doing in Vietnam and how his life was going over there in the jungle. It was tough duty, and I was amazed and frightened for him when I read his letters. He was in the supplies department and had to get supplies to the guys in the field. It was a dangerous job, so I wrote encouraging letters and tried to keep busy while he was gone.

On my way home from Biff Burger one day, I noticed a new store they had been building was finally opening. I saw that they were taking applications, so I stopped in and got one. I filled it out on the spot and handed it back to them, and when I did, they asked me when I could start. It seems they were hiring everyone they could, and since it was better money and a step above Biff Burger, I accepted the offer.

The next day, I had to tell Wendy that I was leaving and say goodbye. She had been so good to me, like a mother I never had, and I really didn't want to leave her.

Our goodbye was emotional, and it was then that she told me she knew I didn't have a home. She had felt sorry for me. But she said she could see how well I was doing and how I had come so far since that day I had asked for a job. She said she was proud of me, and she was thankful she was able to help me. I cried as I listened to her talk to me. When she was done, I told her thank you for hiring me and for taking care of me so well. I told her she had saved my life, and with tears in our eyes, we hugged and said our goodbyes. I told her I would always remember her. She was Wendy, manager of Biff Burger. I don't know that I ever knew her last name, and I never saw her again.

I started my job at the new store, stocking shelves. We all worked hard emptying boxes every day, but it was fun because I felt like I was part of a team. And they treated me like I was part of the team! The job paid a couple more bucks per hour, but I still didn't have enough to buy a car, so I rode my bike.

My seventeenth birthday came and went, and I really felt like I was thirty instead of seventeen. Meeting so many people at the store reminded me that compared to them, I had a different life. The biggest things were that I didn't have doting, caring parents who packed me a lunch. I hadn't gone to high school, hadn't gone to any proms, no girlfriends or boyfriends, no makeup or cute clothes. I hadn't even been taught how to be a girl or take care of myself. I was still tall, awkward, and clumsy. I had been taking care of myself since I was fourteen but really didn't have a mom to teach me anything years before that.

Daddy had told me I was stupid, ugly, and a whore, and those words were the words I believed. I did feel pretty stupid for letting him abuse me for all those years, and I felt ugly because I sure didn't feel or look cute. My legs were too long and hairy, and the hair on my head was wild and curly. I had never been to a beauty parlor in my life. I definitely did not feel like everyone else there at the store, and although people sometimes looked at me twice, no one seemed to really care I was such a mess.

Very soon after I started working at the store, I met Sharon. She was a couple of years older than me and worked at stocking the shelves like I did. We sat and had lunch together every day. She was very perky and had medium-length brown hair that curled around her very freckled face. She was funny and made me laugh, and it was nice to have someone to talk to. She was acting like she was a friend, and that was very strange to me. I didn't remember anyone who wanted to be my friend since Ann Gale in first grade. But I was not complaining; I liked having a friend.

She listened to my stories in amazement and had compassion for my situation, but she could also see I had potential; and for that reason, she decided to help me. It didn't take long for her to realize too that I needed some help being a feminine girl, so she invited me to her apartment. She cut and styled my hair and taught me how to use makeup. When we got our paychecks, we went shopping for clothes, and she helped me pick out some cute outfits. I loved all the attention, and I was really feeling feminine. And it wasn't long before I looked like a decent girl, and it was like being a different person.

Michael O'Brien

It was October 1968 when Sharon invited me to have lunch with her at her boyfriend's apartment, and I thought, *Why not?* We got in her little blue Corvair and drove over to the apartments. Her boyfriend's name was Mike, and he had a roommate named Michael O'Brien, who was also there. They were both in the Nuclear Navy, and their submarine was at the Charleston Naval Base—the USS *James Monroe*. I was a little shy and uncomfortable with Michael O'Brien being there.

We ate lunch at a table on their patio, and Sharon did most of the talking. I didn't say much because I honestly didn't have anything to talk about except my past, and who wanted to hear that? But the guys were fun, and I relaxed and wasn't so uncomfortable.

A few days later, Michael asked Sharon if she and I wanted to come over for a party on Halloween. I was still a bit apprehensive; it was my first "party."

It was a fun party with lots of beer going around. I was not a beer drinker, but I could drink the shots of beer everyone was drinking every sixty seconds. Before long, all of us were giggling and a little tipsy. This was the second time I drank alcohol, and I did not want to overdo it and get drunk. I stopped drinking the beer after we did the sixty-second drinking. Sharon took me home, and I felt pretty good after my very first party!

A couple of weeks passed, and this time, Sharon told me that Michael wanted to know if I wanted to go down to the navy base to see his submarine. I was not sure I wanted to be alone with him. I didn't know him that well, and it made me nervous, and I told Sharon I couldn't do it. But she assured me that Michael was a good guy and that he wouldn't hurt me. She said I would be safe with him. She convinced me I could do it, so I told her to go ahead and tell him I would.

In all my shyness and self-consciousness, Michael picked me up at my apartment. Michael was about ten years older than I was. I was seventeen years old, and I was a recluse from an abusive home. I didn't know if I could pull it off, but Michael seemed to know he had to be gentle and slow with me. He didn't push himself on me or expect me to be someone I didn't know how to be. I was barely learning how to be the girl that I was.

He had a blue 1967 Chevrolet Camaro with a white stripe around the front of the hood, and the engine sounded really good. It was fast, and he showed it off as we drove to the site. We got on base and drove right up to the where the submarine was docked. There was a ladder that crossed the water onto the ship, and it looked scary. But he helped me walk across. He showed me around the parts of the ship that I could see. There was much that was top secret that I was not allowed to see. I was amazed at everything I could see.

When we were done, he took me back to my apartment and asked me if I wanted to come to dinner at his place the next weekend. I hesitated, and he could see my hesitation. He told me he liked me and that he wouldn't hurt me and that Sharon was coming over too, so I timidly accepted the invitation.

By now, I was feeling a little more comfortable around Michael and Mike. They were both very friendly, and when I was there, we spent our time sitting out on their little patio. Michael was very careful about not making it feel like it was him and me. It was always a group environment. But I could see and feel that Michael really "liked" me and was becoming attracted to me. I was feeling really good having a guy who really liked me. Michael was much more mature than me and made me feel like he was a dad-like figure who really cared for me.

Donald Gone

It was November 1968 when Donald came home for a one-month R&R. He came to find me, and I was really happy to see him. He told me everything that was going on in Vietnam and that he had to go back for another year. He told me he still wanted to marry me. I had not been faithful to that commitment even though I still wore his ring. I had to tell him that was not what I wanted. Donald was a friend, and I cared for him. But I really didn't want to wait another year. I didn't feel I could actually do it, especially after spending time with Michael. I told him I had to go on with my life, and I just couldn't be responsible to patiently wait for another year.

He was visibly upset when I told him I couldn't wait another year. It was difficult to explain to him why we couldn't get married, and I knew he would be heartbroken. He just sat calmly and listened, and I could see the hurt in his eyes. I took off the beautiful ring I was wearing and put it in his hand. He looked down at the ring, looked at me, and all he said was *okay* and got up to leave. I stood up too and hugged him and told him I was sorry. He whispered in my ear, "Me too. Goodbye." And he was gone. A few weeks later, I found out he was killed in Vietnam right after he returned, and my heart was sick, knowing he had died with a broken heart because of me.

I told Michael about Donald, and he comforted me and understood the pain and dilemma I felt. I felt so guilty and so bad that I had let him down and hurt him so much. Besides his parents, I was all he had back in the States, and he loved the letters I wrote. He had told me how happy he was when the mail came, and he had a letter from me. I decorated the border of the paper with vines, flowers, and hearts. Just the paper said I loved him, but the words I said did not match the letters I wrote. How would I ever feel right about what I had done to Donald? Michael left me alone until I grieved and got it sorted out and settled inside. My heart still hurts to this day.

It was about a month later, around Christmastime, when I saw Michael again. After we went out a couple of times more, out of the blue, he asked me to marry him. I was surprised but happy that he cared so much. I didn't have a clue how to be a wife. I didn't know how to cook, and I really was just a damaged little girl trying to grow up. We had only known each other for a few months, but I knew he really liked me, and he would take care of me. I would turn eighteen in January, and we got married in March of 1969.

One thing that scared me was that getting married meant Michael and I would have to have sex, and that was something I just did not like or understand. I hated even the thought of someone touching me that way. It almost made me sick thinking about it, and I didn't know how to get "over" that. I told Michael a little about my life and my fears and tried to make him understand we just couldn't do that. He gave me a knowing smile and said, "Don't worry. We will take our time until you are comfortable." I rolled my eyes, knowing I would never be "comfortable." But Michael was very patient and gentle with me. After we got married, I prolonged going to bed as long as I could that first night. When we did, I was completely dressed in a long nightgown with panties and a bra underneath. Michael put his arm over me all night long, and I had a hard time sleeping that way. But in the morning, I felt okay. This continued for about a week. Then we tried kissing a little when we went to bed, and that was not something I was used to either. We ended up just going to sleep that night, and I was sure he must have been angry at me, but he never acted like he was or said he was.

We went shopping and found me some shorty pajamas which were cute and not like my long flannel nightgown I protected myself with. I wore them to bed, and I had my stuffed animal in my arms; and Michael was behind me, spooning and holding me. I finally got used to him being in bed with me and him touching me, but I still wasn't ready to have "sex."

Michael started talking to me about making love; he told me how much he loved and wanted me and that he would always be gentle. He explained that he would never force me and would only do it if I wanted to do it and that it might hurt a little at first, but then it would be okay. I was getting to where I knew I could trust him. I knew he would take care of me and be gentle, and I just felt like I had to let him touch my body. It scared me to death, but after about a month of working around it, we finally made love, and I wasn't scared. It didn't hurt that much. I was still a little uncomfortable, but at least I wasn't feeling like I would throw up anymore. Michael was so kind regarding this and really made me realize that making love really was about loving each other, and it was a natural and wonderful thing.

We found out very soon that I was pregnant and due in November of 1969. I was not sure how I felt about having a baby of my own. I had never thought of having a baby, and it was a new concept to me completely. I don't remember too much of my pregnancy, except that Michael found out that his submarine was being transferred from Charleston to Oahu, Hawaii, in October, a month before our baby was due. He did not want me to be alone, so he arranged for me to fly to Omaha, Nebraska, to be with his dad and mom and have our baby at the military hospital. Michael put me on the plane to Omaha, and then he and the rest of the crew of the USS *James Monroe* took the submarine to Hawaii. I would join him in Hawaii after they arrived in January.

Michael's parents, Jim and Mary Louise, were both kind to me when I arrived. Jim was a sweetheart of a man and really went out of his way to make me comfortable. He could tell I was a little shy and tried to joke around a little to get me out of my shell. Michael's mother was a smoker and had emphysema. I remember watching her sitting in her chair in the living room, smoking cigarette after cigarette and then coughing out her lungs. It was difficult to watch, and she was quite ill.

Jennifer Michelle O'Brien
(November 6, 1969)

On November 6, 1969, I woke up and could feel hard contractions, and no one was there. Michael's sister Anne lived in Omaha, and I called her. She asked me about my contractions, and I told her how I was feeling. She told me I should just walk as much as I could, so I did. There were two doors in the kitchen, one going to the hallway into the bedrooms and one to the living room back into the kitchen. I walked out into the hallway, into the living room, into the kitchen, and into the hallway around and around. I must have walked around this "circle" for two hours, and my water never broke. But my contractions were getting stronger. I was scared to have this baby because I didn't know what to expect. All I heard was, it was supposed to hurt like crazy, and I wasn't looking forward to that.

In the afternoon, the contractions were strong and steady, and they were happening every few minutes. I called Michael's dad, and he came home from work and took me to the Offutt Air Force Base Hospital, where I was to give birth. They checked me into an impromptu room, which was just a place in a hallway with curtains around it. Jim stayed there with me, and the nurses came in and out to check on me. Then one stayed long enough to reach inside of me, and with her fingernail, she broke the water sack. It wasn't long after that my body was pushing out my baby on its own. When her head was showing, which they call *crowning*, they came in and gave me an epidural. This is a shot they give to numb you from your waist down, and it is given with an extremely long needle into the base of your spine. As I bent over in the bed so they could give me the shot, I was afraid I would break my baby's neck. But it didn't.

Now that I was numb from my waist down, they had to tell me when to push, which I did. After about ten pushes, out came that little brown-haired baby girl. They wiped her off a little and then laid her on my chest, and I looked down at the miracle girl, and tears fell from my eyes. I couldn't believe it. What had I done? I had a beautiful little baby girl lying on my chest looking at me. I started crying from the sheer overwhelming emotions of the moment—joy, relief, wonderment, love, curiosity. Jim was standing next to the bed now, and tears were also in his eyes. It was such a magical miracle to give birth to this perfect tiny child. Her dark eyes looked up at me, and my heart surged with love. I couldn't believe I had my very own little baby, but there she lay in my arms—all wrapped up in a pink blanket. And I marveled at her tiny body, and she looked just like her daddy.

They took her away and cleaned her up, then brought her back in to me. They told me two things: don't sit up, or I would get a headache from hell (because of the epidural); and secondly, don't unwrap her. I disobeyed both. I sat up and held that tiny little girl against me and wondered how my body had made this baby girl that belonged to me—a baby girl who would always call me mommy. She would always love me as I would always love her. I tenderly unwrapped her body and inspected and marveled at the tiny fingers and toes. She was all mine, and I couldn't believe it. She lay there looking up at me so peacefully, and I just stared at her for the longest time. My heart filled with pride and love, and I couldn't stop smiling and weeping. I held her close and said to her in a whisper, "Oh, my baby, I hope you have a happy life."

Why, Daddy?

When Jennifer Michelle (Michelle from the Beatles song "Michelle") was about a month old, she and I flew back to Charleston, South Carolina, and we stayed with one of the navy wives whose husband was on the same ship as Michael's. We had no contact with the guys at all, so I guess they just trusted we could and would get across the country and the ocean to Hawaii in about a month.

Before we left for Hawaii, when Jennifer was around eight weeks old, I knew we would in Hawaii for a few years, so I wanted to see my parents and introduce them to their first grandchild. I planned a trip out to Innerarity Point where they now lived. My friend Sharon let me borrow her blue Corvair, so Jenni (her new nickname) and I headed for my parents' house. When I got there, I took Jenni in her baby carrier to the front door and knocked. Daddy opened the door and, without words, let us in. I told Daddy why I was there, and he said Mom wasn't home. I was there alone with my dad. I was a little nervous about being there but really didn't think he was going to beat me or anything. He sat down on the couch (they still had that blue sectional), and I sat down on the couch opposite him and set the baby carrier on the floor next to me. I told him I was married to a navy guy and that we were moving to Hawaii and introduced him to his granddaughter. He just glanced down at her and did not try to hold her or take her out of her baby carrier. I had not planned at all in confronting Daddy about his actions when I was growing up in his house. But there we were, so I got courageous. I asked him straight out, "Daddy, why did you do those things to me when I was younger?"

He looked me in the eye and, without hesitation, said, "Patricia, you are crazy. I never did anything to you."

I sat and looked at him, dumbfounded at what he had just said. I never learned how to defend myself, so I just swallowed hard and didn't know what else to say. I dropped my eyes from his stare and looked down at my baby. I stood up, picked up the baby carrier, and went out to the car. I buckled the carrier into the back seat, walked around the car, paused, and looked at the front door of the house. I didn't see Daddy at all. I got in the car, and we drove off.

Kaneohe, Oahu, Hawaii (1969–1973)

About a week later, I flew out of the Charleston, South Carolina airport with my baby and some other navy wives heading for Oahu. The big 747 gave us plenty of room, and I was sitting next to one of the wives and ended up telling her my entire story, and she sat there listening with tears running down her face. We finally landed in Oahu, Hawaii, and we all stood in line waiting for the doors of the plane to open. When they did, all I could smell was plumerias. We all smiled at one another and couldn't wait to get off the plane and into the sunshine. The air was humid, and it was gorgeous and green from where we could see. There on the tarmac, Hawaiian hula girls danced and welcomed us by putting flowered leis around our necks as we got off the plane. We had to walk from the plane into the building. Michael was first in line waiting for us to come in, and he was so very excited to finally see his baby girl and me. It had been months. He took her out of the carrier and held her so he could see her, and tears flowed from his eyes. She was sleeping, and he marveled at the beauty of this little dark-haired angel that looked just like him.

All the other guys were there to meet their wives too, and it was a glorious day and the beginning of a new start. The guys had rented studio apartments right there in Waikiki, and we all drove to our new living quarters. We could see the ocean from our second-story apartment, and it was an inviting aqua blue that called our names. There were palm trees everywhere, and the sun was warm and comforting.

I knew this was going to be a good place for me, Michael, Jenni, and the other wives and husbands. It was not just beautiful, but I had started to bond with many of the wives as we flew across the ocean. And they sincerely cared about me. It was really the first time I had been accepted by a group of people, and it was doing my heart good, healing a lot of the hurt in my past.

We couldn't wait to get settled so we could go down to the beautiful Oahu beaches. There were about six couples, and we all went together to the beach then we had an early dinner. It was just so exciting to know we were in Hawaii!

Michael was so happy and proud of his new little daughter, and it felt good to see him croon over her. I was happy about this new beautiful place and my new life as a mommy and a wife. I was in heaven, a whole ocean away from my troubled life.

This new little family of mine was almost a shock to my mind. I felt a little disoriented, and I tried to show off by acting like I knew how to take care of Jenni. One of the Navy wives had given me Dr. Spock's baby book, so I was learning. Being married and now having a baby was quite a change of scenery. It wasn't just me and Michael anymore. I was only eighteen years old, and it was like playing house.

For some reason at that time, something made me want everything to be perfect. My house was spotless, and the magazines on the table were fanned perfectly in line with each other. I wanted my house to be perfect—but I think it was that I wanted my life to be perfect. I didn't want a broken life anymore. Being so far away from my mom and dad gave me the freedom to be me, but I didn't know who that was. Now I had a husband and a baby, a perfect little family, and I was determined to keep it perfect. I just didn't know how to do it, so the house was perfect. It was something I could control.

All I could really cook was grits, but I did my best, and Michael helped me. With the companionship and support of the other navy wives, things became easier, and it was starting to feel more natural. Michael always took care of me, and I appreciated that my bad cooking didn't seem to bother him. He was always kind, and I was happy.

After a month in our studio apartments in Waikiki, we started looking for a house to rent. Michael and I found a house on the other side of the island in a little ocean town called Kaneohe. It was over the mountain on the Pali Highway and what they called the "windy side" of the island of Oahu.

The house we found was a two-bedroom, one-bath house, and it had a large covered and screened-in porch they called a lanai. The property was covered with palm and banana trees, and it was located in a small neighborhood. It was a nice house and was perfect for our little family.

All the guys on the USS *James Monroe* were like brothers, and the wives were like sisters. As couples, we spent most of our time with our friends going out to dinner, having barbeques on the beach and parties on the lanai. The guys spent three months at home, then three months at sea.

When the guys were out to sea, us wives spent a lot of time together. The older wives helped the younger ones, including me, grow up quite a bit, and we were like family. We spent most of our time going to one another's homes, going to the beach, and we also went to dinner often.

We girls got to go to a concert now and then, and my first concert ever was Neil Diamond. He was playing at a place called the Shell because the band stand was backed by a huge man-made shell. We all sat in the front row, and we swooned over him as he sang all his songs, including "Sweet Caroline" and "Crackling Rosie." As he looked out at the crowd, I was sure he was singing right at me.

When the guys were home, we had parties on the lanai often. We had a nice stereo system and played all the latest music on our record player—Credence Clearwater Revival, Guess Who, Simon and Garfunkel, Rare Earth, Three Dog Night, Iron Butterfly, Neil Diamond, and the Beatles—and I loved it all. Us girls danced and twirled to the music and had such a fun time. I was enjoying life!

Michael built a bar out of wood and black leather to go on the lanai. One night during one of our many parties, the guys were at the bar putting shots of whiskey on fire and drinking them down while they were still burning. I guess one of the guys didn't drink it down fast enough, and his mustache caught fire; and as the burning alcohol fell on the bar, it caught fire too. He was smacking his face and the bar at the same time to put out the fire, and we all laughed out loud. We had good times on the lanai.

The beaches in Hawaii were beautiful, and we found a nice little neighborhood beach near us called Kailua Beach. One time when we were at Kailua Beach, Jenni was about a year old when I almost drowned her, but it was not on purpose! There was a shallow little pool of water that was created when the high tide came in. When the tide went out, the pool was left. She loved the water, so I put her in this shallow pool in her little round blown-up tube. I turned around to set my towel down on the beach so I could watch her, and when I looked at her just seconds after I put her in, she was upside down in her tube, her legs waving in the air. I ran into the water and pulled her out, and she sputtered a little and then giggled as if it was fun. But it scared me to death!

Another adventure happened one night when we were at one of the wives' apartments to bake cookies for the guys. They had reported for duty but were still on the island. They were just getting ready to leave for their three months out to sea. So about eight of us got together to bake them all a bunch of cookies they could take out to sea.

My friend lived on the second floor of the apartment building, and we all got there around 4:00 p.m. and immediately started making cookies and drinking wine. It was after midnight before we were done, and I was a little tipsy. When I went out to get in my car (Michael's blue Camaro), I walked to the end of the second-story landing and looked over the railing to spot my car before I went downstairs. It seemed the more I looked, the funnier it became because I did not see my car anywhere. I thought I remembered where I had parked it, but it wasn't there. I looked up and down the street and just couldn't find it. I went back to the apartment giggling and said, "I can't find my car!"

The other girls came out, and we all looked over the second-story railing for the blue Camaro, and sure enough, it was gone. We stopped giggling when we realized it had been stolen, and we had to call the police and report it. One of the girls took me and Jenni home. I couldn't believe someone had stolen Michael's Camaro, which was his pride and joy.

The next day, we contacted the base to get a message to Michael, and they said they would tell him. But they were getting ready to take off, so Michael couldn't do anything about it. We would have to wait until he came home. It was less than a week later when they found the Camaro stripped down to the metal in a pineapple field. I was amazed to see the car. There was nothing left on it at all. I don't even know how the police figured out it was the Camaro; there was only a metal frame left. We had insurance on it, so I reported it to them. They provided me with a rental car until Michael came home.

When Michael got home, we bought a bright-orange Volkswagen bug. But after we had the Volkswagen for about two months, Michael saw a 1967 yellow Corvette in a car lot that caught his eye. We drove by it twice a day going to the Pearl Harbor Naval Base, and it wasn't long before Michael decided he wanted it. He said that if was still there on the way home, we would stop and look at it. So that night on our way home, we drove by the car lot, and it was still there. It was a beautiful yellow car with a black hood scoop that said "425" on it, and it was calling Michael's name, "Michael, Michael!" Michael bargained with the salesman until they agreed upon a good price that he was happy with. We left the orange Volkswagen there and drove home in the new Corvette.

That Corvette was beautiful, and it was one of the fastest cars I had ever driven. And one day, Michael decided I might enjoy the powder puff races at our local racetrack. He signed me up. I was only nineteen years old and didn't start driving until I was eighteen, so this was not a good idea.

The racetrack had huge logs about five feet wide on both sides of the first half of the quarter-mile track. The starting gate was run electronically with red, yellow, and green lights they call the "Christmas tree."

We were sitting in the car waiting for the lights to turn green. Michael was riding shotgun next to me, and I revved up the engine, preparing to race. When the light turned green, I slammed on the gas pedal, and we sped down the quarter-mile racetrack easily, beating the other car we were racing against.

In the powder puff, you race three times, and the best time wins; then you get to race the other winners until you get to the two top winners' race. The second time I went, I didn't rev it up as much as you're supposed to, and when the light turned green, I hit the gas pedal, and the Corvette stalled for a second before it took off. I ended up being right behind the other car at the finish line.

Michael explained to me what had happened and said the car had stalled for a moment before it took off because you have to pump the gas pedal and keep gas in the carburetor. So the third time, I was ready. I kept the engine revved up, and when the light turned to green, I screeched out of the starting gate like a real racer and left the other car in the dust. I was in second gear, and we were flying down the track when I pushed it into third gear. That's when I lost control of the car. It spun around four or five times when Michael finally yelled, "Hit the brakes!" I slammed on the brakes, and the car stopped. The car was sitting parallel to the log about five or six inches away. Michael couldn't even open the passenger-side door. We looked at each other and realized we almost died right there. The Corvette had a fiberglass body, and if the car had hit the log, it would have disintegrated into pieces. We sat there amazed and shocked, and I started to cry.

Then the announcer said over the loudspeaker, "The '67 Corvette is disqualified from the powder puff race." And we laughed. After we both gained our composure, I got out of the car and stood there on the track as Michael climbed over to the driver's seat and drove it away from the log so I could get into the passenger side. We drove off the field and went straight home.

After that, the only racing I did was with guys who pulled up next to me at a light and wanted to race the Corvette. I would smile at them like, *Really?* but they sat there revving up their engine. So I had to oblige, and the Corvette always won.

Idaho Falls, Idaho (1972–2009)

Michael and I lived in Hawaii until September of 1972. Jenni was almost four years old when we left. It was so difficult to say goodbye to all of our navy friends. We really had become family. I loved my friends, the wives of the sailors, and we vowed to keep in touch.

The navy shipped our vehicle to Sacramento, California, before we left, so it was there waiting for us when we flew in. We drove the Corvette all the way across the United States to Florida, where my parents and Michael's parents now lived. It took two of the four days to drive across Texas!

We finally made it to Innerarity Point, where my family lived. It had been about five years since I had seen Mom, and she had never met my daughter. I was actually excited to see her. We drove up the driveway, and Mom came to the door and stepped onto the porch. She was standing there, watching me get out of the car; and when she realized it was me, all she said was, "What do you want?"

I said, "Mom, it's me, Patsy."

She just turned and went back into the house. I got back in the car and looked at Michael. "What should we do?"

"We go into the house," he said calmly. "We didn't come this far to leave."

We all got out of the car and went into the house, and my sister Pam met us at the door. She was excited to see us and meet her new little niece. Pam was fourteen, and my little brother, Steve, was sixteen.

Mom had gone to her bedroom and stayed there. That night, after I got Jenni to bed and then Michael went to bed, Pam and I stayed up and talked most of the night. She told me Daddy had divorced Mom recently and that he had gone to live with his first wife, Sarah. I didn't know Daddy had a first wife.

She told me Mom had pretty much abandoned her and Steve and was drinking most of the time. The only meals they got were the free lunches at school. Mom did not buy them food, clothes, or personal hygiene items. The food cabinets were literally bare, so was the refrigerator. There was not even a box of grits to cook in the cabinet. She told me Mom had boyfriends who brought takeout food to the house, and they sat at the table to eat it. But Mom pushed her away when she asked if she could have some of their food. She told me she had to use rags when she had her menstrual period and said she had to wash and wring out the rag and use it over and over again. She showed me her hairy underarms and legs and said Mom wouldn't buy her a razor to shave. She poured out her heart, and it just kept coming. I couldn't believe the conditions these two kids were living under.

The main bathroom was filthy. There was diarrhea sprayed all over the toilet and even on the wall. The rest of the house was also filthy and had not been taken care of, and I found all this to be quite disgusting. So the next day, I went down to Health and Welfare and told them about the situation my younger brother and sister were in. And they assured me they would look into it.

The next day, Pam, Steve, Michael, Jenni, and I went to see my dad in Pensacola. My dad and Sarah lived in a small apartment, and he was lying in a bed and looked like he was dying. Sarah pretty much ignored us and only came in the room when she was bringing Daddy shots of whiskey, which he drank all at once in front of us. Jenni, being a four-year-old, crawled up in the bed with him, and he smiled down at her. I took a picture of her with her grandfather. He was quite sickly, and I actually felt sorry for him. We all gathered around his bed and told him we loved him. It was difficult to do, but he was my daddy. I could see he was going to die soon, and it was the right thing to do. We left his house, and I knew I would never see him again.

The next day, a lady from Health and Welfare came out, and we talked about Pam and Steve's situation. She told us they could put

Pam and Steve into foster homes. Steve didn't want to go to a foster home, and they agreed. He was sixteen, almost seventeen, and was old enough to take care of himself. He had a job, so they thought it best to not put him into the system.

After the lady from Health and Welfare left, Pam and I talked about it, and she assured me she was ready to leave Mom's house and go into a foster home. I thought this was sufficient, so Michael, Jenni, and I packed up and headed for his parents' home in Hernando, Florida. My mom didn't come out of her room at all while we were there, so we left without saying goodbye to her.

The welcome in Hernando was very different than the one we got in Innerarity Point. Michael's dad, Jim, came out to meet us with a welcoming smile on his face. He took Jenni into his arms and immediately started to love on her. After all, he was the first one to see her when she was born. We got our stuff and went inside to a bedroom, all ready for us. It was clean and inviting.

Michael's mom, Mary Louise, had passed away, and Jim was now married again to a very sweet woman named Mamie. Mamie and Jim made a good couple. They were both happy, active, and loving people. They got on the floor and talked and played with Jenni, asking her a bunch of questions. We had a nice visit out on the back porch and then ate a wonderful dinner together.

Their house in Hernando was right on the shore of a lake where there were thousands of alligators. The next day, we took a little boat and putted around the lake where we saw quite a few of them. They would see the boat coming, and they would slide into the water from their sunning spot or just their eyeballs would be sticking out of the water; and when they would see us, they would quickly duck underwater. I had never seen an alligator in real life, and it was fascinating to see them in their natural habitat. When we got back to their backyard, there was an alligator on their lawn. Michael's dad had all of us stay in the boat until the alligator decided to get back in the water. It took maybe fifteen minutes before the alligator must have gotten tired of us staring at him!

We had a great few days with them, and after a wonderful bonding time, Michael and I said our goodbyes and headed for Idaho. As we drove, we talked about my family's situation, particularly Pam's. And we felt like we had made the right decisions and had done the best we could do. I didn't know where Pam was going to be placed, and I didn't have an address for us in Idaho either, so we would have to be out of touch for a while.

Our trip to Idaho was good. We traveled north through Ohio and Illinois, across the plains in Kansas and through Wyoming to the mountains above Idaho Falls, Idaho. It was late September, and the hills around Palisades Lake, Idaho, were in full color, showing off their red, gold, and yellow foliage and the dark green of the evergreens. It was beautiful. I had never seen autumn in the mountains before, and it was a sight to behold. We followed the South Fork of the Snake River into the Snake River Valley and down into Idaho Falls where Michael and I bought a house on Meadow Street.

Michael worked as an operator at the submarine prototype area at the Idaho National Engineering Laboratory. He had a few of his Navy buddies with him there, and we continued to have parties in Idaho with a few of our old friends and some new ones. Michael was not going out to sea anymore, and this was the first time he and I had lived more than three months together.

It was in June of 1973, and I had turned twenty-two in January. It was then that I realized Michael was more like a father who rescued me than he was a husband. Now that may seem like a strange thing to say, but he was almost ten years older, and when I turned twenty-two, he was in his thirties. And he seemed to be so much older than me. I had fun in Hawaii, loved all our friends, and loved being a Navy wife, but something was missing now that we were in Idaho. I didn't know what it was, and I didn't know how marriage between two people was really supposed to be. I just knew something was missing. My heart was yearning for true and honest love, and I wanted someone to be madly in love with me.

Michael was always good to me, and he was a kind and caring man. He was fun, and he was the father of our little girl. He was always a good dad and husband. But I knew if I had grown up in a normal household, and it was time to marry, I probably wouldn't have chosen Michael as a husband. I probably wouldn't have even known him. I found myself wanting something more that would fulfill whatever it was I was missing. Maybe it all had to do with the fact that I was a young girl of seventeen when I met Michael, and I had been pretty much on the run until I met him. I really didn't have any life to speak of before him, but he gave me security and a safe place to grow up. For that, I was and always will be grateful.

Divorce 1

I told Michael my feelings, hoping he would understand, but he was not happy and was even angry with me. He was very hurt that I would consider leaving him, but we got divorced. Jenni and I moved in with a friend named Pat, who lived down the street. She was friends with me and Michael and was doing us a favor since she lived nearby.

To say I had no direction and was a mess would be to say the least. I really had no idea how to live alone as a responsible adult with a child. You would think my life would be adjusted a little bit after being married for five years, but I had no moral compass within me at all. Everything was fly by the seat of my pants, and nothing was too serious. I was committed to nothing. Like divorcing Michael for instance. He was a good husband and a good man, a good dad, and he took care of us well. What exactly was wrong with that? I didn't know. I just knew in my heart that something was missing.

Life at Pat's house was different. She too was a single woman, and Jenni and I settled into her house and got used to living with her. She didn't charge me rent because I did not have a job. Michael gave me child support of $100 per month and a little more on top of that.

Sue and Bobby were also friends of me and Michael's, and I continued to be friends with them. Pat, my roommate, was a little older than me, and Sue was more my age, so I spent more time over at her house. We didn't do much together besides drink coffee at the table in her kitchen, but after my divorce, we became closer friends.

Sue had a brother from Petaluma, California, who came to visit her for the summer. His name was Russ. I was immediately attracted to him. He was good-looking. He had longer brown hair and a cute tanned face. He seemed to like me too; he was more my age. We immediately got along. Sue's husband, Bobby, had a motorcycle that he let Russ ride, and Russ gave me rides up and down the street. Then later he took me for rides in the country. I had my arms around him from behind, and we would fly on that motorcycle. We spent a lot of time together riding, playing, and laughing, and my life was suddenly exciting and fun.

One day, summer was over, and he said it was time for him to go back to California. I was heartbroken and did not want him to go. We were having too much fun together. I begged him to stay, but he said he couldn't. He had to get back to California. After he left, my heart ached for his companionship, and I guess the simplest way to say this is that I lost my mind over him.

Russ went back to his home in Petaluma, California, and I got his address from his sister Sue. With the money Michael was giving me, I bought a ticket to Petaluma and flew to California, took a taxi, and ended up at Russ's front door. His mom answered the door, and I told her I was her son's friend from Idaho. Russ came to the door and was surprised to see me and didn't quite know what to say, but they let me in. His mother said I could stay there one night, but I would have to leave the next day. None of them were too happy about me being there at all. Even Russ was confused and thought I was a little off my rocker, which I was. I was on foot, so his mom took me to the airport and let me off at the departing gates.

I'm not sure what I was thinking, but instead of flying back to Idaho, I got on another plane and flew to Oahu, Hawaii, where I knew Michael's chief and his wife, Darlene, still lived. Darlene had been like a mother to me, and I was good friends with her.

I called her from the airport, and she came to pick me up. And as we drove to her house, she asked me what the heck was going on with me and Michael. I tried to explain and told her I didn't know why I was in Hawaii. I guess it was just familiar territory. I admitted I had made a mistake. I also told her Michael and I had been divorced. And truly, I didn't really know what I was doing.

She asked if she could help, and I told her I probably just needed to get on another plane and go home. She said she would make the arrangements for me, and I could probably leave the next day.

After I talked with her for a while, I called one of our old friends, Gary, and he came over to Darlene's. He asked if I wanted to go grab a bite to eat and talk, so we went to the nearest seafood restaurant and talked about my dilemma and drank way too much. The restaurant was right on the beach, so after dinner, we took a walk on the beach and ended up climbing up into the lifeguard's station to continue our talk, which was a mistake. Luckily, it was late, and no one was on the beach because I got dizzy and felt sick from all the liquor. I threw up over the edge. I was embarrassed, but Gary helped me down the ladder of the lifeguard station. And we went down to the water and cleaned up, and then he took me back to Darlene's house.

The next day, I called Michael and he was shocked that I was in Hawaii. "What the hell are you doing in Hawaii?" he demanded. I didn't know what to tell him. He begrudgingly paid for the ticket to get me back to Idaho. When I arrived in Idaho Falls, he met me at the airport. Michael didn't know what to do with me either. He was deeply hurt that we were divorced, and this was just another crazy incident he didn't know how to handle.

It was very soon after this that things changed again. I went to our house where Michael was still living to visit him, and I found him downstairs in the basement in one of the extra bedrooms, lying on the bed with a gun in his hand. I walked into the room, and he was obviously drunk. He was crying. "I don't know how to do this," he said. "I don't know how to live without you and Jenni." He was waving the gun around and pointing it at me like it was just his finger pointing at me.

I immediately started crying and telling him, "I'm sorry, Michael. I didn't mean to hurt you like this. Please don't do this. You're really scaring me. Please stop it." I was deathly afraid of guns after my daddy had shot through the back window of my "cousin's" car. But I also knew I had to help him and somehow get the gun away from him. He had his finger on the trigger, and as I got closer, the gun went off. The sound in the bedroom was deafening, and a bullet zoomed by my head and hit the freezer. I screamed, and he stopped crying. The sound of the gun going off and my reaction must have sobered him up because the gun fell out of his hand, and he started crying. I crawled up on the bed and snuggled up next to him and told him I was so sorry. It was then that I said to myself, *Who am I to make someone this unhappy?* I had no right and never wanted to hurt people the way I had been hurt.

Michael and I got married again in the Presbyterian church, and we had a wedding party in our basement. All of our friends came, and we tried to make it right again. After the initial excitement of being back together, we got back into the regular grind. It only took a year for Michael to realize I was not happy, and it just wasn't right.

Divorce 2

In 1974, we divorced for the second time; and this time, it was really over. I was twenty-three years old.

Michael bought me an older white Ford Falcon, and I got an apartment for Jenni and me on Mound Street in Idaho Falls. We both slept on one mattress on the floor in the one-bedroom apartment and ate bread and beans for most meals. We were pretty poor, but it was okay. Michael gave us a little more than one hundred dollars in child support a month, but I still did not have a job. Now I had a child to take care of by myself, so we got on welfare and got money from the state to live on.

That helped a lot, and there was also an added benefit of being on welfare: they gave me a grant to go to school. I enrolled in a yearlong secretarial course called office simulation at the East Idaho Technical College. It was structured just like going to a job each day. We had our own desks and phones, and we learned how to type, do shorthand, use the phones, and all general secretarial duties. And we were tested at the end of each week. I really enjoyed this training, and our instructor's name was Kitty, who took me under her wing a little bit.

I met Penny when we were taking the same secretarial course together. Penny was tall and beautiful. She had long strawberry-blonde hair and white teeth. I had long blonde hair and was tall, but I wasn't beautiful like she was. I was still a bit of a wallflower, and compared to her, I was pretty ordinary. She lived in a small two-bedroom house in the country right outside of Idaho Falls, and she invited Jenni and me to move in with her. It ended up being cheaper for us, so we did. Her house was located right next to a farmer's field, and it was nice to live out in the country and to have a friend. It didn't feel like we were trying to make it on our own any longer, and that felt good. Jenni and I took long walks down the farmer's road behind the house and sat on top of the bales of hay and talked about the animals we saw in the clouds. My little girl was my sidekick. She was the only constant creature in my life, and she was such a funny little girl. She filled me with *reason to live*, and we were a team, even though she was still so young.

Bruce Welker Wilcox

In the summer of 1975, I was twenty-four, and Jenni was almost six when we met Bruce Wilcox. Penny and I had been invited by some friends at school to a party at Grassy Banks in Heise, Idaho. Grassy Banks was on the banks of the Snake River. We traveled down the road until we found the place along the river where the party was going on. We pulled up, and right in front of us were two guys drinking beer and talking. Penny and I sat there in the car and looked at these guys. Both of them looked like the hippie type, and they were gorgeous. They both had on bib overalls with no shirt. Both had longish blonde hair, and both had full beards. We got out of the car, and we couldn't help but walk right up to them because they were almost in front of the car.

We said hello and introduced ourselves, and they did the same and immediately started talking to us. Jake seemed more interested in Penny, and I was more interested in Bruce. We all walked over to the keg together, and the guys poured each of us a beer. Penny and Jake walked off together, talking, and that left me with Bruce. He was a talker, so the talking was pretty easy.

We stood and talked for quite a while and sipped at our beers together. I told him I was going to school at the East Idaho Technical College, and he told me he was a carpenter working for a local company. I felt very out of place and almost inadequate talking to Bruce because as he talked, he seemed to be very intelligent. I did not have good self-esteem.

As we were getting ready to leave, Penny told the guys where we lived and invited them to come out the next weekend to visit us, and we offered to make them dinner. They agreed, and later that week, we busied ourselves figuring out what to make them to impress them. I left the cooking to Penny since I was no cook at all, and she decided on stuffed zucchini and salad. That next weekend, there they were, right on time.

We all sat at the big table in the dining room and shared the meal, drinking beer and laughing out loud. I was out of my element and knew I was hanging with some good-looking, cool people and hoped I could hang on for a while. Jenni was there next to me and was the life of the party at times. It was a fun evening, and I felt it went well.

Bruce kept coming by to see me, and he took me and Jenni out to dinner a couple of times. We had been seeing each other for about a month when one day he came over to the house with a camera. He was staying for dinner, and he and I were sitting in the living room just chatting. Penny was busy in the kitchen.

Then Bruce got up and went into the kitchen and started talking to Penny, which didn't seem unusual, but when I got up to set the table, I overheard him asking Penny if he could take pictures of her in the nude out by the hay pile. I heard her giggle and agree to do it, and I stood there in shock, hurt and humiliated.

Bruce came out to the dining room and sat down at the table as if nothing was going on. I went into the kitchen to help Penny get the dinner on the table, and we all ate and made small talk. Bruce could tell I was upset, and later, when we were alone, he asked me what was wrong. I told him, "I overheard you talking to Penny about taking pictures of her in the nude, and it hurt my feelings."

He said, "Why does that hurt your feelings? It is just about photography!"

I told him I just didn't understand why he would think that would be okay with me but that I really didn't want to talk about it anymore.

It had also hurt my feelings that Penny had agreed, and I wondered why she wouldn't say no to him just to protect me. I thought I was her friend, and I wondered what Jake would think of Bruce taking pictures of Penny in the nude. It all seemed so bizarre to me that this would be okay. I knew neither of them knew I had been called ugly most of my life, so maybe I was just overreacting and being supersensitive. I just knew I didn't understand, and I was really hurt.

Somehow we managed to get past that, and we continued dating each other. Six months later, I finished the year at college and graduated with good grades, and that's when Bruce asked me and Jenni to move into his house in Iona.

Bruce's house was a tiny two-bedroom house that belonged to his farmer neighbor Rex. Rex was a kindly old guy, and Bruce gave him twenty-five dollars a week for the place.

Bruce was a good cook, and he taught me how to cook all kinds of dishes and taught me how to appreciate the art of cooking good, homemade food. Good, homemade food is when you use your imagination and your taste buds to create new and exciting meals and not just following a recipe in a book. You can use the cookbook to start a meal, but then you make it your own by adding things you think would be good, or you have a meal at a restaurant and try to recreate it at home.

Bruce, Jenni, and I lived a semipoor but happy life in that little white house. We played games, cooked meals for friends, visited lots of people, went out dancing, and listening to music. One of my best memories was when we used to drive around the dry farm roads. We would stick in a cassette tape and sing our favorite songs at the top of our lungs.

Bruce would open the door of the Suburban and step on the side panel and steer the truck with his toes, and we laughed so hard. We went on picnics by the river and skipped rocks across the surface. We went to the river just to cook dinner and went camping in the back of his old brown Suburban. We stayed up late on Saturday nights, all snuggled up in one another's arms watching *Saturday Night Live* and the *Tonight Show* on a regular basis. And I don't know if I have ever laughed so much.

Bruce was making our lives so homemade and carefree, and I don't think I had ever been so happy. All three of us were hippies together, and we lived life to the fullest. Bruce was a carpenter and made lots of furniture for us, and I learned to sew and made most of our clothes. Bruce almost filled the gaping hole in my heart, but I still had a lot of healing to do. I didn't realize it at the time, but I was still living in survival victim mode.

In February 1976, I got a call from Chip, who told me that our daddy had passed away. I was standing there in Bruce's kitchen, staring out the window, and the only thought I had was, I would never be able to find out why. Why had he done those horrible things to me, and why had he been so cruel to me? I remembered when I had confronted him before I left for Hawaii, and he told me I was crazy, that he had never done anything wrong to me. Now he was dead, and my questions and the apology I needed would go unanswered the rest of my life. I was shocked, devastated, and I cried my heart out.

My brother told me he was going to be buried in the Barrancas National Cemetery, but he added that Daddy's wife Sarah said she would shoot any of us who came to the funeral. The dysfunction continued, so we stayed home in Idaho. Daddy was sixty years old when he died on February 10, 1976.

Biggest Regret of My Life

Bruce, Jenni, and I continued enjoying life together, and then one cold March day, we were driving home from his dad's house when I told him I hadn't started my period and was a couple of weeks late, and I thought I might be pregnant. He pulled the Suburban over and looked over at me with a worried look on his face and sighed deeply. "Patsy, I'm just not ready to be a father."

Those words were my baby's death sentence. We sat in silence for a few minutes. I looked down, and tears began to fall from my face. I knew what I had to do, and I really didn't want to. But I knew if I decided to keep the baby inside of me, Bruce would disappear, and I would have to start all over again alone. I also knew I couldn't raise another baby on my own.

"What should I do?" I asked him, and he told me to see if I could get an abortion.

The next day, I called the hospital, and they told me there was only one doctor who was performing abortions. He was at the hospital in Pocatello, an hour away, and I made the appointment.

Early on April 1, 1976, Bruce and I got in the Suburban and drove down to Pocatello to the hospital. Bruce stayed in the car while I went into the hospital waiting room. They called my name, and my heart dropped into my tummy. I was almost hyperventilating, I couldn't breathe. They put me up on the examining table and propped my feet up into the stirrups. I immediately started sobbing and cried, "Oh my God!" The doctor stopped what he was doing and said, "Are you sure you want to do this?"

I didn't really have a choice. I took a deep breath and said, "Yes." I held my breath, gritted my teeth, and he continued. I felt the tools enter my body, and when he was done, I knew my baby was gone. It only took a few minutes to end a life. I lay there, my heart breaking and hot tears running down the sides of my face. My heart was beating out of my chest, and I felt sick to my stomach. The nurse had to bring a trash can so I could throw up. Then she helped me get cleaned up, and she left the room, leaving me alone.

I sat up on the side of the examining table. Bent over, I put my hands to my face and cried until I couldn't cry anymore. I finally got up, found Kleenex on one of the counters, and blew my nose. I left the room feeling like I had lost an arm or a leg. It was a feeling of great loss, and I was numb.

Bruce was waiting for me in front when I walked out, and I got in the truck, and we drove home in silence. He sensed I didn't want to talk about it. When we finally stopped in the driveway of our Iona house, he asked if I was okay. I told him yes. We went inside and lay on the bed together, and he held me close while I cried myself to sleep.

There is no way for me to change what I did. It was done, and I felt horrible. I knew I had taken the life of a child. I just couldn't get over it, and the regrets are huge. I have never really gotten over what I did.

Sometime after that, we were in the music store at the Grand Teton mall in Idaho Falls, getting Bruce new guitar strings when we saw a concert poster on the wall, saying Fleetwood Mac was going to be in Salt Lake City, Utah, at the Salt Palace, and they were going to be with Firefall. Both groups were my favorites, so we talked about going. We got the number to call, and they still had tickets, so we bought two.

A couple of weeks later, when we got to the Salt Palace arena, we found our seats; and to our disappointment, they were behind the bandstand and behind a big post. Bruce and I sat down and looked at each other, and after a minute of sitting there, he stood up and took my hand and just said, "Come on." We were on the second level, so I followed him all the way to the first level; then we were heading right down the middle aisle, toward the front of the bandstand, until he found two seats open on the left. They were about ten rows from the front. We made our way in and plopped down in the seats, and the view was heavenly perfect!

In about fifteen minutes, a guy yelled over to us from the aisle and said, "Hey, I think you have our seats."

Bruce waved our tickets at him and said, "No, I don't think so. These are our seats." The guy looked puzzled and looked down at his tickets, then left. I don't know what he ended up doing because we never heard another word from him, and we stayed there and watched the most awesome concert from almost-front-row seats.

Fleetwood Mac was awesome. They played every song from their *Rumors* album, and the crowd went crazy. No one was sitting. Instead, everyone was standing and singing every word. It was a beautiful, magical time and such a treat to be able to see Fleetwood Mac at their best and Firefall, whom I really loved at the time.

A few months later, we bought the Ririe Café in Ririe, Idaho, and moved to a little house in Ririe on First Street. Ririe is a farming town of about five hundred people where everyone knew everyone. We were the strangers in town because we were not just new; we weren't Mormon, and they all knew it. Many of the Mormons we served at the café were what they call "Jack Mormon," which means they are Mormon but aren't being faithful to the rules of the church.

We served coffee to the farmers in the morning and breakfast, lunch, and dinner all day long. Our main cook, who was the previous owner, was an older lady who lived behind the café in a single wide trailer. The farmers wanted their coffee early, and if we didn't have the doors open by 5:00 a.m., they would be in front of our house, blowing their car horns to wake us up, so we didn't miss the 5:00 a.m. opening very often.

We made some good food that the customers liked, and Bruce was a talker. We were finally accepted by the little town. We gained some good customers, and it ended up being a fun thing to do for a time. We certainly didn't make any money. The only money I made was tips, and most of the other money we made was for buying food, paying bills, and paying our cook. It wasn't long before our main cook got too old to cook, so Bruce became the main cook, and I was the waitress. And then we were really tied down to the restaurant. And it wasn't so much fun anymore.

Our little house in Ririe was comfortable and gave us two bedrooms and one bathroom that we all shared. Jenni was in one bedroom, and we had the other. Our bed was an old metal double frame with a headboard that Bruce had as a child. We only had the fitted sheet on the bed, and we both slept in one of Bruce's old down sleeping bags that we used as a cover. We zipped the bottom so our feet were snuggled in.

Florida State Health and Welfare finally called, and they gave me the name, phone number, and address of where Pam was living. It sounded like she was living with a good family in Pensacola, Florida. I called the house and got to talk to Pam, who was doing better, and she told us she was being taken care of, which was good news for me.

Bruce and I were really happy together, and it felt like this might be forever. A little over a year after my abortion, we decided it was time to have a child together. We both agreed we did not want to have a baby if we weren't married.

We chose to get married up in Archer, Idaho, in what was known as Grandpa Ozzie's apple orchard. His grandpa had passed away years before, but the family kept the house and apple orchard in the Wilcox family. The apple orchard was white with apple blossoms, and it was so gorgeous and romantic. We invited all of our local friends, and Bruce also invited some of his friends from California.

I made my own wedding dress and wore daisies in my hair, and Bruce had one in the lapel of his cream-colored tux that he wore with his tennis shoes and no socks. One of his friends from California stopped to pick me some yellow wildflowers and wrapped them in tin foil.

We wanted Jenni to be part of the wedding ceremony, so we bought her a tiny, little gold-and-turquoise ring to give to her during the ceremony. We had a *J* engraved in the oval in the middle.

It was a beautiful July day, and we were happy to be getting married to each other.

We went on a long honeymoon trip all the way to Canada. We camped right out of the back of the Bruce's big brown Suburban the whole time and stayed in some very special camping spots, and we danced in the dirt every chance we got.

The first night of our trip, we went to Missoula, Montana, and camped in a little campground. We found out that Crystal Gayle was singing at a bar, so we joined the crowded bar and squeezed into the back of the bar. It was shoulder to shoulder with people listening to her sing. After a song or two, I suddenly got light-headed and completely blacked out. I woke up lying on the floor with people all around me, trying to help. It was a struggle to get me out of there, but finally Bruce got me outside to get some fresh air. By the time I got out there, I was feeling okay but did not want to go back in, so we just went back to our camp.

The next day, we were in beautiful Glacier National Park and pulled up to the Lake McDonald Lodge. Bruce had called ahead to get us a room at Sperry Chalet, but what I didn't know was that Sperry Chalet was five or six miles steadily up on a well-beaten path on a dry, rocky, treeless mountain. I remember looking at the path up the mountain to my right and the beautiful Lake McDonald Lodge to my left, wishing we were staying at McDonald Lodge instead. But even though it was a long grueling climb, it was worth it.

We finally arrived at the top of the mountain, where the chalet was; and the office girls, who looked like real granola girls, showed us to our room. My first impression was how it all looked so stone-cold, but then you hear the story of how they built everything up there from the rock that was at the top of the mountain. The story of the sheer might it took to build it was quite impressive, so we were able to appreciate the effort. The room we got had a nice fireplace that was already lit, and it warmed us up—plus, we both loved a good adventure!

The next day, it took half the time to get down the mountain, so after we made it to the parking lot, at around noon, we traveled via the brown Suburban up the "Going to the Sun" highway and entered Canada and headed for Lake Louise. Lake Louise was beautiful and romantic.

We traveled farther west and got on the ferry that took us to Vancouver Island. When we got there, we took our time and walked through Butchart Gardens in the beautiful city of Victoria. We stopped and smelled at least a thousand roses and flowers along the pathways. It was absolutely gorgeous, and the smell—it was glorious.

We were walking the streets of Victoria, just checking out the store fronts and scenes of the beautiful city when, out of the blue, we heard a loud thump that caught our attention. We looked toward the sound, and that's when we saw the man lying on the sidewalk, blood pouring from his head. He wasn't moving. We assumed the man had a heart attack. Bruce grabbed my hand and hurried me down the street.

We drove out to the beach and drove the Suburban all the way onto the beach near the water and backed up so the rear end of the Suburban was facing the water. We opened the back of the truck and lay on our sleeping bags and pillows looking out on the calm water. Leo Kottke was playing in the background, and we lay there, drinking wine and watching the moon twinkle on the water. There was a long pier that went out almost a quarter mile into the water, and as we looked out at the water and the pier, a fire started at the end of that pier for no apparent reason. The fire got bigger and bigger and lit up the entire sky, and somehow it was beautiful and romantic.

The next day, we rode the ferry back to the United States into Port Angeles, Washington. We went to a grocery store and picked up some fresh king crab legs, some fresh bread, and wine then drove a little farther east of Port Angeles and pulled into a side road. We had no idea where the road went, but we followed it; and deep into the woods, we found one single picnic table and a firepit. We didn't see any signs saying "No trespassing," so we pulled in and turned on the music in our truck, and Bruce built us a fire. We sat side by side on the picnic bench gazing into the fire there in that big green forest. We were having a glass of wine and talking about the fun times we were having.

Just as we were starting the coals for the dinner, Bruce said, "Listen!" and we both fell silent and listened. Then he grabbed my hand and pulled me up, and we started running toward the sound. We were running through the forest so fast branches were hitting our faces, and we were out of breath when we came to an opening where the railroad tracks were laid. We got there just in time as a train came zooming by us going at least ninety miles an hour. The wind almost blew us over, and the sound was thunderous. We laughed out loud, and our hearts were so free, excited, and happy. When the caboose got there, we both stood there and watched the train weave through the forest until it was out of sight. I turned to smile at Bruce, and he was already looking down at me, a satisfied smile on his face.

We went back to our picnic table, drank some more wine, and danced to Firefall in the forest, so happy together—it was incredible. We cooked our crab and buttered the homemade bread and opened a new bottle of wine, and we talked, laughed, and feasted on crab-leg meat until we were full. It was a special night for both of us, and we made the best of it, knowing we were driving home the next day.

The next day, we traveled the rest of the way home to Idaho Falls, and life continued just that way. My life with Bruce was more than good. He was a friendly, talkative guy who talked to everyone. There was never a stranger he wouldn't or couldn't talk to. We would be in the grocery store, and if there was a guy looking for something particular, Bruce would go up and help him find it and give his expert advice on which brand to buy.

Every time he went somewhere without me, he came back with a little gift for me. Sometimes it was a little decorated empty box, sometimes a pack of gum, sometimes warm cashews from the Sears store. Whatever it was, I treasured it and loved that he was so thoughtful of me.

We cooked good meals together, went for walks, rode bikes, and he played guitar for us. We sat and listened as he practiced and played, and we loved his playing. He and Jenni played on the floor together, and he was always doing something to make us laugh. Life with big Bruce was good.

We worked at getting me pregnant, but it wasn't happening easily. I had endometriosis but didn't know it at the time. I found out later that the chances of getting pregnant when you have endometriosis is almost nil. I had very painful periods, and in the middle of the month during my ovulation time, I suffered with the worst pain.

Every month, I prayed and prayed that I wouldn't start my monthly period; and when I did, I sat on the toilet and cried. We really wanted to have a baby, and I also dreaded getting my period because of the pain it caused too.

Jenni was growing up fast. We were still living in Ririe, and she was in second grade. She was a happy little girl and loved going to school. I usually walked up the sidewalk to meet her when she was getting out of school so I could walk her home. One day as we were walking home, she told me, "Guess what, Mommy? I get to be baptized into the church!"

I said "What? What church?"

And she told me that when she turns eight years old, she could be baptized into the Mormon church. I knelt down on the sidewalk so I could talk to her and told her she couldn't be baptized into the Mormon church because we weren't Mormons. She didn't really know what that meant and told me she wanted to get baptized anyway. I told her she would someday, but not in the Mormon church.

When she had her birthday and turned eight years old and did not get baptized, she had to explain to the other little girls she was not a Mormon, and all her little girl friends shunned her after that.

Mormonism was not friendly to us. If you weren't one of them, you were alienated and treated as an outsider. They were friendly enough, but we were never close with any of them. I noticed they liked to brag about the good they did, but honestly the only good done was to their own. And they always seemed to think they were on higher ground than we were because of it.

Natasha Diann (May 23, 1976)

Pam grew up and moved out of her foster home and found a boy-friend who got her pregnant then died in a car accident. Pam ended up with a baby girl she named Natasha Diann (my middle name was given to her).

Pam was living on welfare and living with her boyfriend's mom, Virginia. Virginia did not want to babysit the baby, so Pam tried to find a babysitter so she could go to work. This proved to be difficult for her, and welfare ended up telling her that she either found some-one to watch the baby, or they were going to put her into foster care. That's when she called us. We were shocked but happy to hear from her. We were willing to take care of our niece, so we planned our trip to Pensacola, Florida, to pick her up and bring her home.

When we got there, it was good to see Pam, who hadn't changed at all, and to meet Natasha and her grandma, Virginia. Virginia had a big two-story white house and a yard full of magnolia trees. She had a great big covered and screened porch on the front of her house that was big and inviting, so the next morning, Pam and I took our coffee out there to talk. The sun was just starting to shine through the magnolias, and the sweet scent drifted all around us. It was quite heavenly and so Southern, something I missed.

There was a big couch on the porch, and we sat there in our pajamas and talked about everything that had happened since the last time I saw her. She told me all about the foster home, Dwight (the father of her baby), Virginia (Dwight's mom), and Natasha. Tasha (as we called her) was now nine months old, and she was a beautiful little baby, lots of curly light-brown hair and dark twinkling green-ish-brown eyes. She told me how she was so thankful I had arranged to put her into a foster home, but now, because she was "in the system" and on welfare, how difficult it was to take care of Natasha and have a job to support her at the same time. She didn't want to do it but said her life would just be easier at that time without Natasha. We spent the time relishing in memories, good and bad, and then it was time for us to go. It was very difficult for Pam to say goodbye to Tasha and see her leaving, but even though it hurt, she knew it was for the best.

Tasha was a good baby and traveled well on the three-day trip back to Idaho. When we got back to the house, we put a crib in Jen's room, and it wasn't long before we all got used to her being there, and she became part of our family.

Moving to Lincoln, Idaho

When I was about eight months pregnant, we sold the Ririe Café and bought a house in Lincoln, Idaho, which is on the outskirts of Idaho Falls. This was an older house that had three bedrooms, one bathroom, a big country kitchen, and a woodburning stove in the living room. It had a garage that we never used as a garage, but Bruce used it as his shop where he built beautiful furniture for our house and did some stained glass too. Bruce was very talented and started fixing up our house a little bit at a time. He built a big table for the kitchen, put river rock behind the woodstove, and put stained glass in our front door. He got really good with his stained glass and started to sell it.

From the beginning, Bruce led my life, and I guess that was good because I needed someone to lead my life. Bruce had a very strong personality, and he took control. But he was also very caring for me in every way, and he instilled in me the desire to be home-grown in everything we did. We hardly ever went out to dinner unless it was a birthday or anniversary, so we learned how to cook and entertain ourselves at home. We played games, played with the kids, and always had a puzzle going on the big cutting board he had made. Once a week, I baked bread and a sheet of cinnamon rolls, and I made a yellow cake almost every Friday night. We bought eighty chickens, and after they grew up, we butchered all but twelve, and those twelve gave us eggs on a regular basis. We bought half a beef from a friend who raised them, and I sewed all our curtains and our clothes. The only thing I didn't make were jeans. I hung out our clothes to dry on a line and grew a very large garden of food that I either canned or froze. We were pretty self-sufficient, and I was able to stay home with Jenni and Natasha.

We had Natasha for about nine months, and as she grew up and was becoming a little girl, she was calling me mommy and Bruce daddy because she didn't know any better. And we didn't want to confuse her. We realized it was going to be hard on her and us when she left. She had been a part of our family for almost a year. I began writing letters to Pam to tell her that she needed to come get Natasha because she was becoming too much a part of our family. She never answered, and I didn't have a telephone number for her. But I continued sending letters, trying my best to explain the situation to her about Natasha.

After about four letters, Pam suddenly appeared on our doorstep, and I was so happy to see her. We sat and talked of her life and mine and what her future plans were. She said she wasn't sure, so we talked about options.

I made a nice homemade dinner, and we all sat together and talked as we ate. Then we got up, did dishes, and made some yellow cake together. I think Pam could see the life we were living and how close Natasha was with us. That night after our yellow cake, she decided she wanted to go out to a bar and asked where she could go. I wasn't really sure what she was looking for, but I knew of one place where Bruce and I had gone to listen to country music and dance once or twice, so I told her about that. And she decided to go.

We watched TV for a while and put the kids to bed. After waiting for Pam until almost eleven, we went to bed and did not hear her come in during the night.

The next morning, we found out she never came home but had met a guy at the bar and spent the night with him at his house. It was later on in the morning when she came back to our house and told me she was taking Natasha and going to this stranger's house to stay. I argued with her and asked her why and begged her to not go to this guy's house and take Natasha. I asked her how she could possibly trust this guy she didn't even know, but she didn't want to discuss any of it. She packed up all of Natasha's stuff, and they left together. There was nothing I could do but cry.

We grieved over losing Natasha. She was like our own child, and we hated the thought of Pam taking her to this stranger's house.

But we knew, in the long run, it was better for Natasha to be with her own mom. We had to let her go, and for us, life continued after she was gone.

Bruce built us a firepit in the backyard, and we would cook burgers and s'mores over the fire. Sometimes we would pretend we were camping so we would bring all we needed for dinner and drinks outside and turn off all the lights in the house.

Bruce loved that we were having a baby, so I guess he decided to make it up to me for asking Penny if he could take pictures of her in the nude and asked if he could take pictures of me nude and pregnant.

We drove up on Antelope Flats, where all the dry farms are and found a good, healthy wheat field. We held hands as we walked into the field, and when we got to a good spot, he had me kneel down. And he started taking pictures. The sun was shining on my long braided blonde hair and tanned skin, and my belly was huge with child. He took pictures from every direction until he was satisfied, and the pictures were wholesome, healthy, and beautiful. They actually turned out pretty good. Bruce was a good photographer and had an eye for a good picture. And for the first time in my life, I felt beautiful.

Bruce Ozman Wilcox (October 10, 1978)

I read a book by Suzanne Arms called *Immaculate Deception*, and it taught me all the reasons I did not want to have my baby in the hospital. Our intentions were to have this baby at home. We had regular appointments with our naturopathic doctor and his assistant who was a midwife and was going to attend to the birth.

We didn't know if our child was a girl or boy until it was born, so we had two names picked out. If he was boy, it would be Bruce Ozman after his dad and grandpa; and if she was a girl, it was Sophrona Rose after Bruce's grandma. I drank gallons of raspberry-leaf tea (to build a strong uterus), and we awaited the birth of Oz or Rosy with such great joy.

On the evening of October 9, 1978, I was having slight but steady contractions; and after a light dinner, we rested on the couch. At about 10:00 p.m., we decided we better try to get some sleep because we were sure the baby was coming soon, so we went to bed and slept until about 12:45 a.m.—when I woke up with stronger, regular contractions.

Bruce poured me a hot bath, and I got in, and the relief from the contractions was immediate and wonderful. It was like the water lifted the pain of the contractions off my belly.

While I was in the bath, Bruce turned on Dan Fogelburg music and called the midwife. She was there pretty quick. She gave me a hot tea with cayenne in it to stimulate my blood flow. I had been in the bathtub for about an hour when my body began to go into real labor and started to push out the baby. I didn't want to have the baby in the water, so I got out of the tub and onto the bed. With pillows propping me up, I was inclined, almost sitting up on the bed, and with the midwife directing the show, at 2:14 a.m., on October 10, our son Bruce Ozman Wilcox was born.

The midwife and Bruce in unison said, "It's a boy!" She cleaned him up a little and handed him to me. He was a beautiful baby, with tons of white blond hair, and he had great color. He immediately caught on to nursing, and as he nursed, Bruce sat next to me. We stared at this little creature we had created, and the love was pounding in our chests.

Four hours later, I got up and made a homemade spice cake to celebrate our son's birthday. While I was making the cake, Bruce took the afterbirth and put it into the hole we had dug earlier for the young oak tree we got just for this occasion. Then we prayed for our son, that he would grow up to be as good and strong as the oak tree. We named the tree the Ozzie Oak.

The following song, "Danny's Song," by Loggins and Messina became our life song for the year our son was born.

"Danny's Song,"
a song by Loggins and Messina

People smile and tell me I'm the lucky one,
And we've only just begun, think I'm gonna have a son.
He will be like she and me, as free as a dove,
Conceived in love, Sun is gonna shine above.

And even though we ain't got money, I'm
so in love with you, honey,
and everything will bring a chain of love.
And in the morning, when I rise, you bring a tear of joy to my eyes
and tell me everything is gonna be all right.

Seems as though, a month ago, I was Beta-Chi,
Never got high. Oh, I was a sorry guy.
And now, I smile and face the girl that shares my name.
Now I'm through with the game. This boy will never be the same.

And even though we ain't got money, I'm
so in love with you, honey,
and everything will bring a chain of love.
And in the morning, when I rise, you bring a tear of joy to my eyes
and tell me everything is gonna be all right.

Pisces, Virgo rising is a very good sign, strong and kind,
and the little boy is mine.
Now I see a family where there once was none.

MY LOVING DADDY

Now we've just begun.
Yeah, we're gonna fly to the sun.

And even though we ain't got money, I'm
so in love with you, honey,
and everything will bring a chain of love.
And in the morning, when I rise, you bring a tear of joy to my eyes
and tell me everything is gonna be all right.

Love the girl who holds the world in a paper cup.
Drink it up, love her and she'll bring you luck.
And if you find she helps your mind, better take her home.
Don't you live alone, try to earn what lovers own.

And even though we ain't got money, I'm
so in love with you, honey,
and everything will bring a chain of love.
And in the morning, when I rise, you bring a tear of joy to my eyes
and tell me everything is gonna be all right.

Oz was the delight of our little family, and he was such a good baby and didn't give us any trouble. Every morning, Bruce brought him into our bed, and Oz would nurse as we both went back to sleep. We had so many wonderful times with our new baby boy.

When Oz was about two years old, we went to Grassy Banks with some friends for an Easter picnic. The firepit we found had been there for years, and the area surrounding the pit was worn down so far. The pit was high, and the dirt slanted downward away from the pit. So our short beach chairs were inclined back away from the fire. It was comfortable for a while, but then somehow Oz, who was just a toddler at the time, came up the incline and accidently tumbled backward into the fire. I screamed and tried to jump up to get him out of the fire but could not get out of my chair because of its backward incline. His baby hands were in the red-hot coals, and he was struggling to hold his tiny blonde head up above the coals. Our friend Bret, who had come with us, immediately realized what was going on and came on a dead run to the firepit where he grabbed Oz and jumped to the other side of the pit and headed for the car.

We rushed him to the hospital where the doctor examined his burned little hands. He had to clean the wounds before he wrapped them up, and that was the second time that day my precious baby was in so much pain. To have my little guy hurt like that just about killed me. I was angry that this had happened, and I blamed myself. I couldn't grasp the helplessness I felt when I couldn't get out of the chair. I still cringe at the thought of that incident.

It was a few months after this ordeal when we decided to go down to New Orleans, Louisiana, to visit my family. Jen was about ten, and Oz was two. We met up with Steve, Annette, and their first child, Dennis, in New Orleans, and then we all caravanned the three hours to Pensacola, Florida, to meet up with Pam, her husband, Steve Ortega, and Natasha, who was about seven, and Chip. I had not seen Chip for years and was so happy to see him. This was the first (and last) time all four of us kids—Chip, Steve, and Pam, and I—were together since we lived at home. All of us stayed in one motel room right on the beach in Pensacola, Florida, and our bodies covered all the beds and every inch of the floor. It was such a hysterical adventure. We spent the day playing on the beach and making memories and loving on each other.

The next day, we went to Fort Pickens, where they had imprisoned Geronimo, who was an Apache war chief in 1886. We went to the actual cell where he was kept, and there on the floor was a lone brick lying on the floor. I picked it up and looked it over and thought about Geronimo touching this brick when he was in prison, and for some reason, I put it in my purse, knowing it was against the rules, but there it was. And I just had to have the keepsake. I later found out I am one-sixteenth Indian. I still have that 129-year-old brick, and every time I see it, it reminds me of when all four of us kids were together again and for the last time.

There was a tunnel that we attempted to follow. It was made of concrete, and the top of it was only about waist high, so we were all bent at the waist. Chip led the way into the wet, dark tunnel; and before long, we all got claustrophobic. But we couldn't turn around, so we all had to back out backward. The whole time we were laughing hysterically as we made our way out.

Afterward, Pam took us to the trailer she lived in with the man she had married, Steve Ortega. The living room in the little trailer was full with all of us—Steve Ortega, Natasha, Bruce, Oz and Jen, me, my brothers Steve and Chip, and my sister, Pam. The four of us kids sat around, savoring the time we had together and reminiscing about our own past and memories. We took a funny picture of our very similar Ward feet, which were just big feet with long toes.

We took another picture of all four of us standing together, and it was funny to realize I was the shortest one of all my siblings. All my life, I always felt like I was the tallest among my schoolmates, and here I was with my family, and I was the shortest of all four of us. Chip was five feet eleven; Steve, six feet five; Pam, six feet; and I was, and still am, five feet seven.

We didn't want it all to end, but we finally had to say goodbye. After lots of hugs and tears, Jen, Oz, Bruce, and I left and drove back to Idaho.

Our family always had fun when we were on road trips together. We played all kinds of activities on the road, like I spy with my eye or slug bug or the alphabet game where you had to find something outside that started with the next letter of the alphabet. It wasn't quiet very often, and when it was, it meant both of them were asleep in the back seat.

When we got home, I heard of a contest on our local radio station to win a trip to Hawaii, so I entered the drawing. I would have loved to take Jen, Oz, and Bruce to Hawaii. And for some reason, I was sure we would win the trip. The day came when they were giving away the trip, and we all listened intently. The second-place prize was a waterbed, and after they announced the winner for the Hawaii trip, and it wasn't me, I told Bruce and the kids, "Just watch, I'll win that stupid waterbed."

And the next thing the announcer said was, "Patsy Wilcox wins the second prize, the waterbed!" I was speechless!

We went to pick up the prize, and again we were surprised. The waterbed was really nice. It had a wooden frame with shelves and cabinets in the headboard, and we were so excited about our new bed that we actually forgot about the trip to Hawaii.

You May Know Who He Is, but You Don't Know Him

After I had Oz at home, I became really interested in home birth, so I went to a home-birth seminar, and there I met another home-birth enthusiast named Debbie. We became friends and got together often to talk about lots of things, including home birth—the pros and cons.

One day, we were having lunch together, and we were sitting out in the backyard with our sweet tea. We were talking about all kinds of stuff, and I ended up telling her my life story. After hearing my story, she finally said, "Patsy, you need Jesus in your life!"

I looked at her and was a little offended, and I told her, "Debbie, I was raised Episcopalian. I know who Jesus is!"

She smiled at me and said very gently, "You may know who he is, but you don't know him."

This took me by surprise, and I said, "What do you mean?"

And that's when she told me about Jesus. She went out to her car and got a little pamphlet that showed the great divide between humans and God and how Jesus bridged that gap to God's open door.

That night after everyone went to bed, I sat in the living room in my rocking chair in front of the fireplace and read the pamphlet. The truth of his sacrifice and resurrection opened my eyes to see Jesus for the first time. This information went from my head straight to my heart, and I cried my eyes out, realizing what Jesus had done for me.

I found Debbie the next day and told her I had read the pamphlet, and we talked for hours about the sacrifice Jesus made for us. I was very emotional, but the whole thing started to make more sense to me. And there was a dim light finally turning on in my brain; it was the first step of saving my life.

I didn't realize at the time how emotionally damaged I was. The little girl who had been sexually, physically, and physiologically abused was still there, so there was quite a bit of healing to be done.

But he had been there all along, and now it was becoming clear. It was a beginning.

Going to Church

Debbie invited me to go to church, so my family met her at the Assembly of God church in Idaho Falls, Idaho. We sat in the pews feeling a little uncomfortable because it was not something any of us were used to, especially the singing. It was a feeling of inadequacy because everyone seemed to be connected but us, but Debbie gave us her knowing and understanding smiles, which made it not so bad.

The pastor gave a good message, and when we left, a smiling man at the door said to me, "God is going to bless you!" I was like, *Okay, whatever that really means.*

We went to that church for a few months, and I learned more and more about Jesus and God. Then the pastor and his family moved to Texas, and the assistant pastor took over. His main concern seemed to be the new church building they were building, and it didn't seem so good anymore. I really loved the sermons the previous pastor had given us. It seemed he had a personal relationship with Jesus that I really admired.

So somehow we felt brave enough to seek out another church. Debbie had a friend who was attending a small church in Idaho Falls called Family Bible Church, so we decided to give it a try and loved it. The services were on Sunday mornings in a movie theater, and the pastors were Rick and Cheryl Lunsford. The music was different; it was loud and seemed to be motivating! I found myself crying during many of the songs, and Pastor Rick's sermons were good. I cried through most of them too. God's love was really getting closer to my heart.

Amy

Right after we got settled in this church, we met Amy and Randy through one of the couples we went to church with there. Our friends were camping at a campground right outside Idaho Falls called Table Rock campground. While they were there, they met the people who were camping right next to them and found out they were traveling from Illinois and did not have a home. They were living in a tent at the campground with their young daughter, Carmen. When our friends found out these people were pretty much homeless, their Christian hearts knew they had to do something. They knew us pretty well and thought this little family was much like our little family, so they brought them to us.

We welcomed Amy and Randy and their daughter, Carmen, into our home. Carmen was about the same age as Oz, and Jen took her on like a big sister. They all started playing immediately, and Amy and I became friends right away too. She had a "gypsy" heart just like mine.

Randy and Amy stayed with us and Bruce helped Randy get a job as a carpenter. After a month or so, they found a house on the Ririe Highway, and they moved. We spent quite a bit of time with them and got to know them pretty well. I found Amy to be a very mothering type person, and she was kind. We became really good friends.

Amy was pregnant when they moved into the house on the Ririe Highway, and when it was time to have her baby, she really considered having it at home. I was going to help deliver, but Randy wasn't totally on board for this, and I was glad because I was not experienced and had never delivered a baby. If anything had happened to her or the baby, I couldn't have lived with myself. So when it came time, Amy gave birth to Patricia (my namesake) in the hospital.

Amy and her family attended church with us at Family Bible for a while, and we grew as close as sisters as we learned about Jesus together.

My friend Debbie had a friend named Debbie P., so me and Amy and the Debbie's started a Bible study together. The study we were doing was called Seven Stars, and it was based on the book of Revelation and the Old Testament laws.

We girls wanted with all our hearts to follow and obey God. We all quit attending the Family Bible Church and had church at our house. We all dug deeper and deeper into the Old Testament and tried to apply more and more rules to our lives so as to please God. We all started observing Sabbath as Friday night when the sun went down until Saturday night when the sun went down. I even learned how to make the unleavened bread called challah, and my family endured this as they tore the unleavened bread and dipped it in wine before dinner every Friday night. I think my family must have thought I was going way overboard on this "religion" stuff, but they never said anything.

Then one day our new friend Debbie P. was giving all of us girls a ride home. We drove along chatting about our Bible study, and when we got to my house where Amy and I were getting out, Debbie P. turned around from the driver's seat and summarized our chat and looked at Amy and me with this evil look in her eyes and said, "Anyone can say they are a Christian." We weren't sure what she was talking about, and just the way she looked at us, it was almost like a demon talking to us.

Our hearts were beating wildly as we got out of the car, and we couldn't get inside the house fast enough. When the door shut, we looked at each other. It was like a light went on. What were we getting ourselves into? It scared us both, and we sat on the couch and talked about what she had said and this legalism we had gotten into. We realized we had left Jesus out of the whole equation of our Bible study. We decided we would not go to the Bible study anymore, and we were going to learn more about Jesus. I told Debbie that we couldn't do the Bible study anymore. We wanted out, and soon we lost touch with both Debbies.

By then, it was too late. Randy had gotten so sick of us being wrapped up in the legalistic stuff that he thought I was a bad influence on Amy and moved his family to Swan Valley, where he started drinking and smoking pot, and things really went downhill from there. Randy didn't want me around Amy, so I wasn't able to visit her in Swan Valley, which hurt my heart. Before too long, Randy was being verbally abusive to Amy and the girls. He left them for weeks at a time with no food or money. Amy cleaned a woman's house so she could feed her children. That woman was like an angel to Amy.

Randy's brother Tom lived in Sun Valley, Idaho, and was troubled by Randy's actions and was worried about Amy. He finally went to Swan Valley to rescue Amy and the girls and brought them to my house. Amy contacted her brother Ben in Prescott, and he flew to Idaho Falls to take Amy and girls to Arizona.

It was so difficult to say goodbye. Amy was like my sister, and I loved her and her girls. But we had to say goodbye to each other. We hugged and cried together, but they had to go. I cried as I watched the yellow Subaru leaving our driveway taking my best friend to Arizona.

Years later, Amy married Scott, and he had two children, Matthew and Summer. Amy became the mother they never had, and together she and Scott loved all the kids and poured God's love into their hearts.

On February 21, 2002, when Matthew was twenty-four years old, he was killed by a drunk driver who went through a red light. I can't put into proper words how this devastated the family. It was the most horrible thing that could have happened, and Amy and Scott and the kids took it hard. Matthew was such a kind and giving young man who had such a wonderful future ahead of him. It was a tragedy that will never end.

When I found out, I did not know what to do or say, but I knew I just wanted to be there for Amy. But this was a family tragedy.

There was nothing any of us could do but grieve with them and pray for comfort.

Matt's death was still relatively fresh when Amy came to Idaho about a year later to attend a Women of Faith with me. We traveled together down to Salt Lake City, Utah, where the conference was to be held. Amy poured her heart out, and I let her cry and tried to comfort her. She told me she could barely see the next step in front of her. She was confused and angry at God. She didn't understand how something like that could happen.

Women of Faith is a Christian-based live-events organization that stages nondenominational events across the United States. It was always an awesome experience that I looked forward to each year, but this one was extraspecial. I was praying that God would speak to Amy and help her because I didn't know how. She is my very best friend, my sister in Christ, but I did not know how to do anything but pray and hope I could gently point her back to the only one who could help her—God.

Amy and I checked into our hotel room, and after getting settled, we headed over to the venue. We got on the elevator to go down the six floors. We were alone in the elevator when it stopped at the third floor. Sheila Walsh stepped onto the elevator. Sheila Walsh was one of the main five speakers at the Women of Faith. I recognized her immediately. I also knew this was a God-appointed moment in time. Just like the friends who lowered their friend from the roof of a house Jesus was in, I felt I needed to tell Sheila about Amy and her heartache. Sheila listened, and with tears in her eyes, she hugged Amy and prayed for her.

Later, when Sheila was on stage speaking to the twenty-five thousand plus women, she said, "I have a special message for the woman I met on the elevator today. She is in here somewhere, and God wants you to know that he hears your heart."

I grabbed Amy's hand as Sheila continued, "You can trust God with your deepest pain."

Amy cried, and I could see how broken she was. I cried and prayed, *God, please help her.*

The message Amy received that weekend was the beginning of her way back into his arms. There have been so many valleys and mountains to climb since, then but God gave her these scriptures:

Psalm 30 (New Living Translation)

I will exalt you, LORD, for you rescued me.
You refused to let my enemies triumph over me.
O LORD my God, I cried to you for help,
and you restored my health.

You brought me up from the grave, O LORD.
You kept me from falling into the pit of death.
Sing to the LORD, all you godly ones!
Praise his holy name.

For his anger lasts only a moment,
but his favor lasts a lifetime!
Weeping may last through the night,
but joy comes with the morning.

When I was prosperous, I said,
"Nothing can stop me now!"
Your favor, O LORD, made me as secure as a
    mountain.
Then you turned away from me, and I was
    shattered.

I cried out to you, O LORD.
I begged the Lord for mercy, saying,
"What will you gain if I die,
if I sink into the grave?
Can my dust praise you?
Can it tell of your faithfulness?
Hear me, LORD, and have mercy on me.
Help me, O LORD."

You have turned my mourning into joyful dancing.
You have taken away my clothes of mourning
    and clothed me with joy,
that I might sing praises to you and not be silent.
O LORD my God, I will give you thanks forever!

Psalm 31

O LORD, I have come to you for protection;
don't let me be disgraced.
Save me, for you do what is right.
Turn your ear to listen to me;
rescue me quickly.
Be my rock of protection,
a fortress where I will be safe.

You are my rock and my fortress.
For the honor of your name, lead me out of this
    danger.
Pull me from the trap my enemies set for me,
for I find protection in you alone.

I entrust my spirit into your hand.
Rescue me, LORD, for you are a faithful God.
I hate those who worship worthless idols.
I trust in the LORD.
I will be glad and rejoice in your unfailing love,
for you have seen my troubles,
and you care about the anguish of my soul.

You have not handed me over to my enemies
but have set me in a safe place.
Have mercy on me, LORD, for I am in distress.
Tears blur my eyes.
My body and soul are withering away.

I am dying from grief;
my years are shortened by sadness.
Sin has drained my strength;
I am wasting away from within.

I am scorned by all my enemies
and despised by my neighbors—
even my friends are afraid to come near me.
When they see me on the street,
they run the other way.

I am ignored as if I were dead,
as if I were a broken pot.
I have heard the many rumors about me,
and I am surrounded by terror.

My enemies conspire against me,
plotting to take my life.
But I am trusting you, O LORD,
saying, "You are my God!"
My future is in your hands.
Rescue me from those who hunt me down
    relentlessly.
Let your favor shine on your servant.
In your unfailing love, rescue me.

Don't let me be disgraced, O LORD,
for I call out to you for help.

Let the wicked be disgraced;
let them lie silent in the grave.
Silence their lying lips—
those proud and arrogant lips that accuse the godly.

How great is the goodness
you have stored up for those who fear you.

You lavish it on those who come to you for
    protection,
blessing them before the watching world.

You hide them in the shelter of your presence,
safe from those who conspire against them.

You shelter them in your presence,
far from accusing tongues.

Praise the LORD,
for he has shown me the wonders of his unfailing
    love.

He kept me safe when my city was under attack.

In panic I cried out,
"I am cut off from the LORD!"
But you heard my cry for mercy
and answered my call for help.

Love the LORD, all you godly ones!
For the LORD protects those who are loyal to him,
but he harshly punishes the arrogant.

So be strong and courageous,
all you who put your hope in the LORD!

That was my very brave and courageous friend Amy. I'm so
proud of her, and I thank God that she came to Women of Faith that
weekend. I thank God that he spoke to her and helped her.

In the meantime, Bruce and I went back to Family Bible
Church. Our pastors Rick and Cheryl had a friend they brought with
them from California. His name was Mark. He was quite a radical
believer, and he was also a musician. Bruce grew to like him because
he was a musician too. They played music together and enjoyed get-

ting to know each other and their music. Mark played guitar and played mostly Christian music he had written. Bruce wasn't a singer but played beautiful Leo Kottke-type music, which is fancy finger work on the guitar using a glass slider, and my favorite was "In Christ There Is No East or West."

Bruce had quite a few guitars, one being a Martin, which is a very finely made guitar. He also had a beautiful banjo that was inlaid with pearl, and one day Mark asked Bruce if he could borrow his banjo. Bruce, of course, said yes and let him take it. It was more than a month later when Bruce remembered Mark had not returned his banjo yet and that he hadn't been around lately, so he asked Rick where he was. The news was not good. He found out that Mark had fallen off the wagon and had gotten back into drugs and alcohol, so he had gone back to California. He was gone, and sadly, so was Bruce's banjo. Bruce later found out that Mark had sold his banjo for drugs. It really broke Bruce's heart, and he was angry and regretful that he had trusted this "Christian" friend.

Bruce told me he had it "up to here" with Christianity, and he was done with my legalistic religious antics, Randy's turn to drugs and abuse of Amy and the girls; then Mark stealing and selling his banjo was the final straw. Bruce didn't want to have anything to do with so-called Christians after that, and I really didn't blame him. He didn't trust them, so we stopped going to church. I needed the fellowship, the Word, and church, but he was angry and bitter. We found ourselves going down different paths—Bruce was running away from Christianity, and I desperately needed it and was trying to find it.

By the time Oz was six, we were drifting further away from each other. And then I started feeling that old familiar emptiness in my heart. I was confused about religion, and something was missing. And I didn't know what it was. Bruce and I used to have a good and happy marriage, but now things were different. We were not the old Bruce and Patsy who sang songs together as he drove the Suburban with his toes.

The following song described my heart at the time, and when I heard it, I cried.

Total Eclipse of the Heart, a song by Bonnie Tyler

Turn around, every now and then I get a little bit lonely
And you're never coming round
Turn around, every now and then I get a little bit tired
Of listening to the sound of my tears
Turn around, every now and then I get a little bit nervous
That the best of all the years have gone by
Turn around, every now and then I get a little bit terrified
And then I see the look in your eyes
Turn around bright eyes, every now and then I fall apart
Turn around bright eyes, every now and then I fall apart

And I need you now tonight
And I need you more than ever
And if you only hold me tight
We'll be holding on forever
And we'll only be making it right
'Cause we'll never be wrong together
We can take it to the end of the line
Your love is like a shadow on me all of the time
I don't know what to do and I'm always in the dark
We're living in a powder keg and giving off sparks
I really need you tonight
Forever's gonna start tonight
Forever's gonna start tonight

Once upon a time I was falling in love
But now I'm only falling apart
And there's nothing I can do
A total eclipse of the heart
Once upon a time there was light in my life
But now there's only love in the dark
Nothing I can say
A total eclipse of the heart

Turn around bright eyes, every now and then I fall apart
Turn around bright eyes, every now and then I fall apart

And I need you now tonight
And I need you more than ever
And if you only hold me tight
We'll be holding on forever
And we'll only be making it right
'Cause we'll never be wrong together
We can take it to the end of the line
Your love is like a shadow on me all of the time
I don't know what to do and I'm always in the dark
We're living in a powder keg and giving off sparks
I really need you tonight
Forever's gonna start tonight
Forever's gonna start tonight

Once upon a time I was falling in love
But now I'm only falling apart
And there's nothing I can say
A total eclipse of the heart
A total eclipse of the heart
A total eclipse of the heart
Turn around bright eyes

I loved Bruce with all my heart and wanted us to be like we had been
so badly. My heart was breaking, and I was totally lost and without

130

hope that we could ever be there again. The enemy was trying his best to convince me our love was over, and Bruce wasn't trying to convince me otherwise.

Bruce was the first man I truly fell in love with and felt we chose each other. We had a beautiful baby together, and we were soul mates. He pampered me and treated me like his woman. We laughed, loved, and grew into adults together. We were so happy and had such a beautiful relationship. I knew he was madly in love with me. Bruce was twenty-four, and I was twenty-three when we met. I know that if we had continued with our search for Jesus together, we would still be together. He was my everything, but I was still the damaged little girl.

The Beginning of the End

When Oz started school at Lincoln Elementary, I decided to get a part-time job. There was a meat-cutting and wrapping business in the back of the little quick stop right on the corner near our house. One day, I asked if they needed any help, and they said they needed someone to help wrap and hired me on the spot. This was when and where I met Dee.

Dee was single and was rough around the edges. She was a tough-leader type, knowing exactly what she wanted, and she wasn't timid. We talked as we worked, and we told each other about our own lives. We became friends quickly.

Then one day, she asked me if I wanted to go out with her after work one night. Bruce and I didn't go to bars and hardly went out at all. Mostly, it was out to dinner on our anniversary, his birthday, or mine. I wasn't really into going to bars, but I thought it might be okay because I would be with her, and we could just have a drink. And it was a good chance to talk. I asked Bruce if he minded, and he said, "No, go ahead."

She was divorced from her husband, and their two young sons lived with him in Challis, Idaho, which was a few hours away. She seemed to be needing a friend, so when she asked me to go out again; and after the first time, I just told Bruce I was going out with Dee.

We went out a few times, and one time when we went out, I saw a friend of mine and Bruce's at the bar sitting at a table alone. It was Steve. I told Dee I would be back in a minute and went over to talk to him. He was not sober, and it was only 6:00 p.m. He started crying when he told me he and Mary Jo had gotten divorced, and he was heartbroken. I felt very sorry for him and could understand now why he was not sober. We talked for a while, and he explained what had happened.

Steve and Mary Jo had gotten into cocaine, and Steve couldn't give it up. They had two young children, so she kicked him out of the house when it got out of control. Both of them were good friends of ours, and I was surprised to hear this information. Because they were friends, I felt like I should help if I could; and because I knew him, I felt safe with him. But when he asked if I could come back to the bar the next night, I hesitated because I didn't really want to go out two nights in a row. But Steve was really hurting, and he was a friend, so the next night, I went to the bar without Dee and met Steve there.

I was kidding myself that I could be of any help. Steve was a drug addict, and I had no experience with that at all. I felt sorry for him and just tried to help, but after a couple of weeks of seeing him, pretty soon I realized he had sucked me into being his only friend.

I talked to Dee about him, and she could see he was using me and advised me to stop befriending him no matter what history we had as friends.

The final straw was when he wanted me to be more than a friend and tried to talk me into going to his place to fool around, and that was when I knew I needed to break it off. He and his addictions were more than I could handle, so I told him I was sorry. I had to say goodbye.

The last time I saw him, he called my house from the phone booth outside the corner gas station, and he was so drunk I couldn't believe he had been driving. I walked down to the corner and found him passed out in his car. He had vomited in the car and was now lying in it. His car was filthy and smelled horrible, and I wasn't about to clean it up or wake him up. I just left him there and hoped he would stay passed out until he could drive. I never saw him again.

San Francisco

Bruce and two other guys got a contract to build some condominiums in San Francisco, and it would take them a few months. We both thought the separation might help us. After they were there for about a month, they invited us wives to join them in San Francisco, and we were excited to go.

It was the middle of summer in San Francisco, but it sure didn't feel like it. We were cold! This was my first time in San Francisco, and I didn't know I should have brought warm clothes. Bruce and I went shopping for a warm sweater I could wear. We had fun walking around Frisco, holding hands and visiting some of the shops, and we had a fresh dose of "happy" seeing each other. I was really hoping this trip to San Francisco to see Bruce would be the turning point for our marriage, and it seemed it was so.

During the first month the guys were in San Francisco, they had met a young girl who had sailed a big wooden sailboat all the way from England to San Francisco all by herself. She offered to take us all out sailing around the San Francisco bay on her sailboat, and everyone was all for it. We made plans to meet early the next day.

That night, we went to a fancy seafood restaurant where we ate king crab legs served by a waiter in a black tuxedo, and I felt pampered. I'm sure the guys had spent time figuring out the best things they could do for us girls, and I have to say they chose well. We had a delicious dinner and spent the evening drinking wine, laughing together, and having fun in San Francisco.

The next day, we all went to the dock to meet up with the sailor girl and boarded her sailboat. When I met her, I was immediately intimidated and too shy to talk to her, but big Bruce didn't have that problem. She was a cute girl and had short messy brown hair and was maybe five feet tall. Her skin looked like brown leather, and she was salty and tough. I looked at her and thought she was crazy and way braver than me.

It was chilly in the morning, and though the sun was warm, it remained chilly all day, especially because we were getting sprayed with water from the wind in the bay, so we were a bit wet. The way the boat was rocking and rolling was making everyone else a little seasick, so they all went down below and remained sick most of the day.

Bruce and I stayed up top and enjoyed the experience of it all, and sailing in the boat was awesome. We tried to eat the sandwiches we brought, but before we got two bites, the bread was soggy from the mist.

I couldn't imagine how this young woman had managed to cross the sea in her sailboat all by herself. She told us sailing stories about other long trips she had taken into warmer waters, and she had sailed all over the world. She was an amazing person, and I surely wished I was a little bit like her. Although, I could never see me sailing a boat across the ocean by myself. It was a once-in-a-lifetime experience for all of us, and we thanked her with all our hearts. By the time the day came to an end, we hugged goodbye like good friends

We girls flew back to Idaho Falls with some good memories of San Francisco.

Bruce called and told me how much he enjoyed our visit and that he loved and missed me. He was ready to give our marriage his best shot, and I was too. We talked every night, and a couple of months later, he came home.

I was happy to see him, and we tried to make things right. We truly loved each other, but I knew how flawed I was and also knew how much I needed Jesus. I wasn't free to talk about my search for Christianity, so I felt like I was concealing part of my heart. I needed more. I needed healing. I needed God. I had to make a choice.

We sat down to talk and I tried to explain that I loved him, but we weren't on the same page any longer. I wanted to pursue a relationship with Jesus, and he didn't.

Another thing was that I had lost sight of me because I seemed to be suffocating under Bruce's strong personality. Bruce always had a very strong personality and self-confidence. He was able to talk to anyone, but my lack of self-esteem from my own upbringing had kept me from keeping up with him. After a while, I felt like I was becoming invisible. It was like I didn't have an identity. I wasn't Patsy; I was Bruce's wife. I didn't know how to change that. It would mean changing who Bruce was, and that was not possible.

I didn't feel like I could do it anymore. This was who Bruce was, and my heart was broken.

One day he came home, and we sat outside by our firepit in the middle of the day and talked about the situation. We talked about our wonderful life, the beautiful son we had given birth to, the wonderful daughter we shared, the fun times we had, our honeymoon, and driving the old Suburban with his toes.

He always took care of us, always loved me, was always kind and thoughtful, and he was a good dad and husband. He never neglected, never abused. I had been his girl that held the world in a paper cup and made his dreams come true. But he and I both knew that something was missing, and it was like we had gone too far to go back again. Neither of us knew what to do. We were lost without Jesus in our lives.

Ending this marriage was going to be difficult for all of us. Bruce didn't want to live without us, and we weren't sure we wanted to know how it would be to live without him. It was a terribly sad thing just to think about, and we cried because we knew it was almost over.

Holy Spirit Visit

We stayed together for a few more months, and during this time, I was feeling so very sad and empty. One day, Bruce had taken Jen and Oz out shopping with him so I could stay home and take a nap. It was a cold October day, and I snuggled into the couch to watch an old movie that would usually put me to sleep. I pulled a light blanket over my body and got the television remote and switched the channels until I found an old black-and-white movie that I thought would do the trick.

The movie was about a little boy who was about six years old and sadly had been dropped off at an orphanage by his parents because they didn't want him anymore. The boy stood on the steps of the orphanage and watched as his mommy and daddy drove away, and it was clear he was not completely understanding what was going on. The orphanage director tried to get him distracted, but his eyes were glued to the back of the car as it drove away. The director took the child inside and showed him to a room decorated for little boys. The child sat down at the foot of the bed, and his feet didn't touch the floor. Alligator tears started falling from his eyes. It was obvious he was in shock and was scared.

The orphanage director tried to talk to him, but he just stared out into space at nothing and refused to even talk. There was a window in the bedroom, and he spent most of his days standing next to the window looking out at the driveway. The realization slowly came that his mommy and daddy weren't coming back, and the heartbreak showed in his eyes.

One day, the orphanage director got him to take a walk with him outside; and as they walked, he held his hand and talked to him about all the beautiful things they saw on their walk like the trees, flowers, and the sunshine.

They sat down under a big shade tree that looked down at a creek gently flowing, and they sat quietly just listening to the water running over the rocks in the creek. Then the director began talking to him. He said something like, "I'm sorry your mommy and daddy had to leave you here. I know you miss them very much. Sometimes mommies and daddies don't know how to take care of their little boys. But I know somebody who loves you very much. His name is Jesus, and you know what? He promised he will never leave you, and he will always love you."

The little boy looked up at the director with his sad eyes, and tears began to fall from his eyes. The director continued to talk to him, telling him about the love of Jesus.

I don't remember much of the movie after this because when he started talking about the love Jesus has for us, my heart started thumping and yearning for that same kind of love. I began to cry as I identified with the little boy. It was the first time I had witnessed the same kind of heartbreak that defined my own tragic past, and it touched a place in my heart. When my parents began to drink so heavily, they forgot about their kids. All that was important to them was found in that bottle of Jim Beam.

The devastation in my heart overwhelmed me, and there I was, sobbing uncontrollably like a baby. And that was when God, in the form of His Holy Spirit, came to me. In my very emotional state, I felt something/someone lie down behind me and put his arms around me. Then he whispered in my ear, *Patsy, I love you, and that is all that matters.*

In my thoughts, I said to him, *But what do I do about my daddy?*

His answer was quick and true. It was the only truth that could set me free. He said, *You have to love and forgive him.*

Love and forgive him? But he never admitted or apologized for what he did to me. I had never thought of forgiving him first before he said he was sorry; and now that he was dead, how could he? Love and forgive him?

But somehow I knew God's advice was right, and I said, "Yes, okay." And he gave me the strength and good sense to forgive my daddy, and immediately I felt love and sympathy for him.

Ephesians 6:15, in the Message translation, says, "Wake up from your sleep, climb out of your coffins, Christ will show you the light."

I felt like I had been heading down the wrong road and definitely heading for destruction. I was only twenty-seven, and I had two failed marriages and two children by different fathers. And who knows what my future would have been because I had no idea how to live life on my own. Would I turn to drugs or alcohol in my future? I didn't know and really felt like I had one foot in the coffin. But God saw me in my despair. He felt compassion for me and bent down to lend me his hand, and he helped me sit up.

I slowly stood up in my coffin and looked at him in amazement and believed every word he said. It was like Jesus turned the key to the lock that was hooked to dozens of chains that wrapped around my heart. When the lock opened, all the chains dropped to my feet, and I was free. It was such a cleansing moment when all the weight of the bitterness, unforgiveness, and heartbreak fell off me. God's true, pure love filled my heart, and it was a supernatural moment.

When he helped me out of my coffin, I stepped into a beautiful kingdom full of light. My spirit soared and mingled with his. And for the first time in my life, I felt good, loved, clean, peaceful, and happy.

It took the power of a loving, merciful, caring, and kind God to speak healing into my life. It was strange, but it seemed like the little girl inside of me became healed and set free too. My mind was clean and clear, and I felt great joy. It was like a heavy rain had washed through my mind, and now it was clean and fresh. Have you ever experienced a heavy rain, and when it was over, the sun came out, and the smell of fresh rain just made you smile?

I later realized this was when I was filled with the Holy Spirit, and I became a new creation. I started a new life that day, at that moment. My old life, my old baggage, my old heartaches were all gone. I truly felt like a brand-new person. It was an immediate change from darkness to light. It's like I had been in a dark room, and someone turned on the light. Or I lived in a cave all my life, and one day the rock that held me in rolled away, and there was a blinding light. I finally realized, he was all I ever really needed—he is the light and the love.

Divorce 3

I told Bruce about my experience, but it didn't seem to affect our personal relationship. We both knew we couldn't turn around at that point. And because Bruce loved me, he set me free. Oh, if I had only found the Lord earlier, Bruce and I would probably still be together. He was my soul mate.

We had an attorney friend who was handling our divorce, and as we walked from the car to his office, we held hands. When we went into his office, he saw our tears as we sat there holding hands, and he stopped what he was doing and told us, "You know, you have to have a good reason to get a divorce." And we told him we did. He shook his head, as if to say, "How sad," and wrote up the divorce papers, "Irreconcilable differences."

The afternoon, Bruce moved out. The kids and I were devastated. He put all his stuff in the old brown Suburban and left. The kids and I got on my big empty bed and cried ourselves to sleep. I felt like I had made the biggest mistake of my life, and my heart felt lost and empty. I didn't know what to do. I was sincerely sorry.

The kids and I continued to live in the house, and Bruce paid the mortgage payment. Eventually, we got into a routine of living without Bruce. I did not have any close friends at church and didn't want to go alone, so I was not attending church regularly. Even so, I knew God had changed my life, and I could feel his love in my heart.

I got a job working as a salesperson at a popular radio station called KLCE and met a new friend, Linda. She was single, so we hit it off right away. She tried to help me sell advertising, but it wasn't long before I realized being a salesperson was not my cup of tea. I just wasn't good at talking people into buying advertising on the radio station. The final straw was when payday came, and I didn't get a commission check. I started looking for another job.

One day, I was at the Peppertree restaurant having lunch with my friend Linda and her friend Georgeanna, and we were just chatting about different things. I told them about my job at the radio station and how I didn't get a commission check, and so I was looking for a new job.

Georgeanna worked for a real estate company and attended luncheons that the local Idaho Falls Chamber of Commerce sponsored and told me they were looking for an administrative assistant, and she thought I would be perfect for the job.

She didn't know I had not even graduated high school. I filled out an application, and she put in a recommendation. The only real work experience I had was wrapping meat at our corner gas station and failing at selling advertising at the radio station, so I was not sure why they would hire me. I didn't have high hopes, but then I got a call. They wanted to interview me right away, so I made arrangements to interview with the fifteen board of directors (at once), and lo and behold, they all liked me. I was offered the job as the chamber's administrative assistant. I was amazed that they actually wanted to hire me, but I accepted the offer, and off I went.

This job meant I would work closely with Del Brewster, the executive director. Del and I met every morning and went over his schedule. And every day he added more for me to do, and I was learning step by step. I took care of the membership, received their dues, and kept the books, mended relationships with disgruntled members, set up the Tuesday luncheons, and got some interesting people to be speakers. It was a fun job with a lot of responsibility, and we were also very involved with the city of Idaho Falls and worked closely with the mayor.

Wick

Bruce and I had been divorced for about a year when I met Wick. Dee and I had joined a women's pool league, and she was teaching me how to play pool at a bar called Pockets because it was a bar that was full of pool tables (pool tables come with six pockets for the balls to roll into).

Wick and some guys were there that day, playing pool, and Dee noticed him and told me the little that she knew about him. He was one of the best pool players in town, and he was divorced. I looked over at him, and he seemed like a cool-looking dude, maybe a little intimidating. After I thought about it for a while, I walked over to where he was and sat down next to him. He looked over at me and smiled, and I introduced myself and told him I was told he was one of the best pool players in town. And in a humble way, he laughed it off. He was about my height, maybe an inch taller. He had long thin hair he pulled back into a ponytail, and he was distinguishingly handsome.

Wick and I started seeing more of each other, and he invited me to a party at his house. I met many of his friends, and they were all laid-back people, nice enough, and me being Wick's new sidekick didn't seem to affect them at all.

Wick had a cabin up in the mountains, and on the weekends of the summer, we went to his cabin and floated the river in his aluminum drift boat. We didn't fish, and we always floated the same area of the river. In the winter, we did a little bit of cross-country skiing on the weekends, and this was usually with some of his friends.

One thing I noticed about Wick was that he was a man of habit. We did the same things in winter and summer on the weekends. We never went out to dinner, never made dinner together, never went to a movie, or did any shopping together. But for some reason, he was like a boyfriend to me.

I had no intention of getting married again after Bruce and I separated, so I felt safe with Wick. We had a simple relationship that would never amount to anything, and that was fine with me.

In between my time with Wick, Dee and I hung around; and once in a while on weekends, we would go up to Swan Valley, Idaho, to go dancing at the Saddlesore Saloon where there were always great live country rock bands playing. Dee and I danced with anyone who asked us to dance, but my favorite dancing partner there at the Saddlesore was Macki. He had his own way of doing swing, and I could follow him with ease, so he liked to dance with me too. We had so much fun dancing!

One night, we got up to the Saddlesore; and after a while, Dee told me she'd had a little too much to drink and didn't want to drive home. She was going to stay overnight with a friend and that I needed to find a place to stay as well.

I went up to the bar, and I knew everyone sitting at the bar, so I asked them all at once if there was anyone who could spare a piece of floor I could sleep on that night. And the bartender, whom I didn't know, told me I didn't have to sleep on the floor. He had a bed I could sleep in anytime! I looked at him like he had just slapped me in the face and laughingly told him, "No, thank you!"

Sharon and her husband, Rich, who were sitting at the bar told me I could sleep on their floor, so at the end of the night, that is whom I went home with. I didn't know at the time, but that bartender would end up being my husband.

After a couple of years, Del left the Idaho Falls Chamber of Commerce and Idaho Falls to take on a bigger Chamber of Commerce position in California, and I was put in charge as the acting executive director position and ran the chamber for a little over a year. It was not much different than what I was already doing, so it was easy to do. I met with the board of directors on a regular basis, and they seemed to be pleased with my performance. I was making good money, and I was happy with my situation. It still amazed me that I had no education, and the only experience I had was wrapping meat and barely selling advertising for a radio station, and here I was, running the Idaho Falls Chamber of Commerce.

Kery Wyn Secrist

It was right around May 1986 when a nice young man from the March of Dimes visited the chamber office. He came into my office and asked if the chamber would be interested in sponsoring (and arranging) an event to raise money for the March of Dimes called Bid for Bachelors. After a brief discussion, I told him we would be happy to and thought it would be fun for all, and we signed the agreement. Me and my friend Linda got to work arranging a place to hold the event. And then we had to put together available bachelors and date packages.

We had fun and came up with some great ideas, including airplane rides to Sun Valley, Idaho, and Jackson Hole, Wyoming, and hot-air balloon rides as well as quite a few "dinner and a show" dates. All we needed was a bunch of bachelors, and because both of us were single and knew a lot of business owners, we knew quite a few. We got the word out, and the single guys started coming out of the woodwork.

Linda and I were in the Sandpiper Restaurant and Bar to talk to Ron the manager about getting some donated dinners from his restaurant, and he was happy to do it and went to his office to get our gift certificates.

As we were standing in the foyer waiting, Linda said, "Oh, look, there's Kery Secrist. He is single, and he would be a good one. Plus, you would like him because his mother is into herbs." I wondered why she thought that herbs would matter to me, but I guess I was a granola girl.

We walked up to the bar where Kery sat alone at the bar, and he was intently reading a Louis L'Amour book.

Linda told me she had been best friends with his sister Debbie, and I immediately recognized him as that bartender at the Saddlesore Saloon who had offered me his bed so I didn't have to sleep on the floor. She introduced us (formally), and I was feeling a little uneasy talking to him. I wondered if he recognized me from the Saddlesore.

We told him all about the Bid for Bachelors and how it worked and asked if he wanted to be part of it. At first, he told us no, that he would be too humiliated if no one bid on him. We both assured him that we would bid on him, and after some deep consideration, he said he would do it.

We were happy we had one more bachelor, and we continued setting up the date packages until the night of the event. We had about three weeks to go.

Wednesday night finally came around, and the bar was full of girls ready to bid on some available bachelors. The guys got up on stage one by one, and the announcer described what date package went with each guy.

The bidding was going well, and everyone was having fun. Then Kery got on the stage, and things changed for me. I was pleasantly surprised to see him standing there, slim and tall in his black cowboy hat, white long-sleeve shirt tied at the neck with a black bolo tie, black jeans, and cowboy boots. He was looking good, and I blinked twice and swallowed hard. I swear I had never seen anyone clean up as well as he did. He got my full attention.

The bidding started, and I only hesitated for about five seconds. Then I raised my own flag to make a bid for him. The bidding continued, and I thought many others were bidding on him because the price was going up fast. I raised my flag for him again and again. Then I found out there was only one other bidder on the other side of the bar. She stood up to see who was bidding against her. And when she saw it was me, she yelled at me, "Patsy, what are you doing?"

I recognized her as a girl I knew from the chamber and felt embarrassed that I hadn't even considered he might have a girlfriend. I sheepishly laughed as if it wasn't a big deal, and I'm sure I turned red when I said, "Sorry! Okay! I'll quit bidding." And I immediately stopped bidding. She made one last bid and won him, and for me, any ideas about him was over.

Thankfully, the bidding started for the next guy and needed my attention, so I quickly got back to work. Kery walked by in front of me and smiled up at me, and I tried to pretend I didn't see him.

We finished out the night and ended up making thousands of dollars for the March of Dimes, and everyone was happy. I went home thinking about what a fool I had been to even consider that Kery would give me a second look and wondered what I had been thinking and finally just let it go.

Much to my surprise, a few days later on a Friday night, my phone rang, and it was—well, guess who? I smiled to myself and got butterflies when I heard his voice. He asked me if I was interested in floating the river in his drift boat the next day, and I was a little bit shocked. I asked him if he was sure about this, and when he said yes—well, he didn't have to ask twice. I loved floating the river, and I told him, "Yes, I would love to." He said he would pick me up in the morning. I asked if he needed directions, and he said no, he knew where I lived.

The next morning, Kery showed up. When he came in the house, he asked me if I remembered him coming to this house before. And I was like "What?" He told me he had been our real estate agent when Bruce and I had tried to sell the house. I was surprised that he knew who I was, but I didn't know him. We loaded up into his truck and headed to Swan Valley.

I didn't know how to fish or row, so I just sat in the boat, getting suntanned as he fished. We spent the day together, and we chatted easily and comfortably. It felt good. I was a bit intimidated by him because he seemed to have it all together, and he seemed to be a little arrogant. I assumed he must have lots of girls after him since he was the main bartender at one of our more popular bar/restaurants.

The next weekend, he called me again and asked me if I wanted to go float the river again. He said, this time, he would bring a fishing rod for me so he could teach me how to fish. Well, I liked the idea, so we floated the Snake River and went fishing. We had a great day.

The Idaho sunshine was so warm, and the scenery on the river was beautiful. It was very enjoyable and peaceful.

Then he asked me to come down to the Sandpiper where he worked because they were having a band playing that he thought I might like. Well, I like any kind of live music, so I went and sat up at the bar by myself. The music was good. Kery paid for my drinks and spent his breaks sitting by me, enjoying the music, and talking to me.

Wick and I got together the following weekend and played some pool together at the Crown Bar, where we saw some friends, and we hung out with them for a while. Then we all left and went to his house to listen to some Bob Dylan and have some drinks.

Then Kery called to see if I wanted to go float the river again, and I said I would. We had another great sunny day, and I got back into the fishing mode. I even caught fish, which was fun!

We were spending a lot of time together, and he was showing a great interest in me and me in him. And it wasn't long before I realized I had a problem I never imagined I would ever have, and that was, I had two "boyfriends" at one time. Being in that predicament made me feel quite uncomfortable.

I felt like I was doing something wrong behind both Wick's and Kery's backs and didn't quite know what to do. Wick and I had a good, free, and open arrangement, and I knew he would be okay with me seeing someone else just to have fun, but maybe not getting serious with them. And I didn't think Kery would appreciate it if he knew I had this "relationship" with Wick, but we didn't have any kind of serious relationship to consider.

Well, Wick had done nothing wrong that made me want to change my situation, and this thing with Kery had kind of been an interruption and could lead to a future I wasn't sure I wanted. I knew I had to make a decision, and I finally did.

I called Kery and asked him if we could have lunch together that day, and he agreed. We met at the Sandpiper. When we were seated, we sat facing each other, and I began to explain my predicament. I told him I was starting to have feelings for him, but I was still with Wick and had been for two years. I didn't like how it made me feel, like I was cheating on both of them. And I had come to a decision about what to do, and it just seemed right that staying with Wick was the fairest thing to do.

Staying with Wick was also the easy decision as I knew what to expect, and I knew we both liked our current situation. I didn't have to be rejected if Kery decided he didn't really like me. I didn't have confidence in our current relationship and wasn't sure that Kery would ever really want me, so I gave him up. But secretly, I really hoped he would fight for me or try to talk me out of it or call me, but he didn't. He just let me go as easily as he had found me, and that made me realize I had made the right decision.

Wick and I kept seeing each other just like we had in the past. About a month after I broke up with Kery, something happened that made me reconsider. I had spent the night at Wick's house, and the next morning, he got up and made his regular microwaved scrambled eggs; then he got on the phone and started calling a bunch of different girls who played golf to set up a game for later that day.

I wasn't a golfer and probably wouldn't have gone anyway, but for some reason, this hurt my feelings. I realized that I was just another one of Wick's "girlfriends." We all had a purpose in his life. Like tools, he took each out when he needed it. I had a feeling I may have given up a good thing in Kery, and I guess I also realized there was no real future for me with Wick.

I explained how he had hurt my feelings. He didn't seem overly concerned about it all but did say he was sorry it hurt my feelings. But for some reason, the incident meant more than we both realized, and I told him goodbye and left his house.

Something inside of me had changed, and living in this uncommitted relationship was not working. I guess I realized I might like having a guy who actually wanted to take me out.

It took me a month to clear my head and start over again. I really liked being single and got back into the groove of taking care of me and the kids and enjoying a simpler life. But I couldn't seem to get Kery off my mind.

One More Chance?

After things settled, I really started thinking about Kery and realized I must have had feelings for him because I was thinking about him constantly. But I was hesitant because I remembered he hadn't done anything to try to keep me but let me go so easily like I didn't matter. Well, I knew I needed to matter, so I wasn't sure if I should pursue him or not.

I decided to test the waters and finally got the courage to call him one night. I asked how he was doing, and we talked for a while. Then I timidly asked him if he was interested in going on a date with me. He paused for a minute and finally said, "Are you sure this is what you want to do?"

I said yes and waited for his reply. He finally suggested we go out for dinner to talk, and I agreed.

He picked me up, and we went to a Mexican restaurant we both liked and sat across from each other. We talked about what had happened and what would prevent a similar breakup, and I told him I was not with Wick anymore. I tried to explain how things had gotten so complicated when I was involved with both of them.

We started dating again, but this time, something was different. Maybe he didn't fully trust me and was keeping me at an arm's distance. I couldn't quite put my finger on it, but something was different; I could feel it. This time, it wasn't as exciting as losing him at a bid for bachelors' event and him coming back like a knight in shining armor to win my heart. This time, he wasn't trying to win my heart. It was almost like I was forcing my heart on him. After all, he didn't call me. I called him.

On our third date, we were driving to Swan Valley to go float the river in his boat; and as Kery was driving, he reached into his jacket and pulled out this little vial that had white stuff in it. I looked down at it and knew it must be cocaine; then he offered it to me. I immediately said, "No, thank you," and sat there wondering what I had gotten myself into. Nothing else was said. He just put it away, and we continued to drive down the highway, both of us in our own thoughts. Mine were wondering what I was supposed to do next. It seemed to me that he had lost respect for me and didn't care what I knew about him, or he was trying to scare me away. At the moment, I decided I would ignore it and hoped he wouldn't offer it to me again.

We continued dating, going out for dinner, going floating, and hanging at the Sandpiper, and no sign of cocaine ever came up again.

Kery had a really good friend named Marshall, and he was dating a girl named Joanne. One day, Joanne told me how confusing it was for her to see Kery dating me because according to her, Kery already had a girlfriend. She was Joanne's friend from Albuquerque, Kathy. She was an airline stewardess who saw Kery each time she came to town. Then it was me who was confused. I thought maybe that was why Kery was keeping me at an arm's distance, and I braced myself for the letdown and thought, *Well, what goes around comes around!*

You Are Smart!

After I had been the acting executive director for the Idaho Falls Chamber of Commerce for a little over a year, they finally hired a new executive director, and it was time for me to move on. I remembered that Bruce had talked to me about getting a job at the Idaho National Laboratory because they paid well, and the benefits were great. But I would have to get a GED diploma since I didn't graduate.

I contacted the Eastern Idaho Technical College (EITC) because I knew they gave the GED tests. I made an appointment to take the tests a week later. I got to the college, and a nice lady showed me into a room where I could take the tests. I sat down and looked them over. The tests covered things like math, English, and history. I was a little intimidated because the last grade I attended was the eighth grade in Charleston, South Carolina. She told me there was no time limit, so I just started reading each question and gave the best answer I could.

When I was finished, I gave my answer sheets to the lady, who took them into her office to grade them, and I sat down in the waiting room. The sign outside her office said she was the college counselor at EITC, and her name was Patricia Heubner.

It didn't take long for her office door to open, and she came out holding my test scores. She sat down next to me and, with a smile, said, "You did great!" and showed me the test scores.

I was shocked and couldn't believe it. I told her I had quit school right after eighth grade started, and she just shook her head and smiled and said, "Well, you have great scores here, and you are very smart. These scores are above average. You really should consider going to college!"

Tears welled up in my eyes as I looked at the "above average" scores. My heart was doing flip-flops, and I really was choked up and speechless. She could see the emotion I was going through and put her arm lightly around my shoulder. She really had no idea the impact her words had on me. Being called "stupid" much of my life was so drilled into my mind that hearing those words was almost confusing. But after I swallowed hard and thought about it, I was the one who took the test, and I was the one who got above-average scores. I accepted them in my mind and replaced the word *stupid* with *very smart*. It took years to make the change, but I finally realized I may not be "very smart," but I knew I wasn't stupid anymore. Thank you, Patricia Heubner.

After I found out about Kery's girlfriend Kathy, I was not quite as open and trusting with him as I had felt before because I felt he was hiding something from me. He didn't tell me about her. Our relationship was not a "madly in love with you" relationship but more of an "I like you but I'm not sure I can trust you" relationship. But for some reason, we kept on dating.

I met his family during Christmastime. His sister, Debbie, and her family lived in Pocatello, Idaho, and were having a family Christmas party, and Kery took me. I was very shy around his family, who all seemed to be happy and outwardly loving people, and they seemed to like me.

We dated pretty regularly but lived in our own separate homes and lived our "single" lives. I got a job working in the secretarial pool at the Idaho National Lab, and Kery was still working the bar at the Sandpiper and was also selling real estate. Dee and I went to the Saddlesore once in a while, and Linda and I went out now and then for a drink.

Jen was sixteen at this time and got tired of being Oz's babysitter, so she moved in with her dad, Michael, and his wife, Kay Lynn. Oz was eight years old and in second grade at the Lincoln Grade School.

Kery and I had been dating for about six months when I asked him if he was interested in maybe getting married one of these days. I guess I was testing the water because I really wasn't sure what he thought about our relationship. I didn't really want to get married, but companionship was appealing, and it would be nice to have someone "take care of me." I didn't have a lot of faith in my ability to be a good wife, but maybe being madly in love wasn't necessary. Kery was a decent guy, and he seemed to have a level head and stability. He was smart and proud and a little bit arrogant, but I also saw a tenderhearted man when he took care of his mom, and he loved dogs.

On Valentine's Day in 1987, Kery and I went to the Sandpiper to have dinner. We were both dressed up for the occasion, and Ron, Kery's friend and the manager of the Sandpiper, came by to take our Valentine's Day picture.

When we finished eating dinner, we sat and chatted over a glass of wine. Kery kept reaching into his coat pocket and finally took out a little box. He opened it and showed me a ring and said, "I love you. Will you marry me?"

I was surprised and felt more afraid than happy at the moment. I didn't trust myself, and I knew he didn't realize there was doubt in my heart, but I said yes, and we set the date—April 11, less than two months away.

I invited my best friends Amy and Dee to be my maids of honor, and Kery's dad came from California. Kery's friend Reed from the Sandpiper was his best man. My former pastor agreed to marry us.

We gathered at one of Kery's friends' house in Swan Valley, Idaho, on the shore of the South Fork of the Snake River. We had planned to have the ceremony outside next to the river, but it was spring in Idaho, and it was too cold and wet that day. We got married inside the house next to the warm fireplace.

I wore a white cotton dress with puffy sleeves and brown cowgirl boots, and I had wildflowers in my long hair. Kery looked handsome in his boots and black hat. Jen and Oz were dressed up and stood next to me.

We had our wedding reception at the York Grange in Idaho Falls. We hired a local band to play for us, and we all danced and had a great time.

Marriage on the Rocks

Our marriage started out good together. Me and the kids moved into Kery's house, and we tried our best to figure out a new life together. Our days were filled with floating the river, fishing, and drinking gin and tonics. The gin and tonics on the river tasted like lemonade and quenched our thirst. During the week, Kery made us gin and tonics each evening, and we were tipsy most of the time. Kery was a drinker, I guess because he worked at the Sandpiper, and everyone bought him drinks. But I wasn't used to drinking that much, so I didn't handle it well.

I was used to Bruce being very loving and kind to me, and Kery's indifference and arrogance was more than I could handle at times. He thought he knew everything, and he thought he was always right. He would make everything a competition or retaliation. He was not kind, loving, or caring to me, and that was exactly what I did not need. His pride made him my enemy instead of my lover, so it wasn't long before we were at each other's throats. His arrogance rubbed me the wrong way and made me boil with anger because I didn't understand why he treated me so badly, like I didn't know anything about life in general. Everything was an argument. He blamed it all on me, and of course, I blamed it all on him.

Most of our fights were about how to raise Oz, who wasn't easy to raise, but Kery was too tough on him, and he had no patience or grace with him. Of course, Kery thought I was too easy on him, so we argued. I just figured that because Kery never had children of his own, he didn't have that unconditional love that parents have for their own children.

And drinking habits didn't help us at all. The more we drank, the more we fought. After a few drinks, the arguing was out of control. We would say anything, true or not. Just lots of ugly words thrown at each other and the so-called love we had for each other dwindled as our dislike for each other grew.

One of our fights almost drove me over the edge of sanity. We were yelling at each other for hours, and after some especially harmful words about me being a failure as a mother, I just gave up and didn't want to fight anymore. At that moment, I didn't want to live anymore either. I felt so defeated, so worthless, and such a complete failure as a human being.

I had done it. Just like I had feared, it seemed I had ruined another marriage. I had already failed two men who had put their trust in me to love them for richer or poorer, for better or for worse, and I had two children who were directionless because of my lack of ability to be a decent mother. And now this marriage was quickly going down the drain.

I went into the bedroom and sobbed until I couldn't cry anymore. Exhausted, I got up and went into the bathroom to blow my nose and wash my face. When I looked at myself in the mirror, I saw a broken, damaged girl who didn't have a clue how to live life, and it seemed all hope was gone. I opened the medicine cabinet and saw a few bottles of painkillers and aspirin, so I took them all out of the cabinet. Kery was in the living room, sitting on the couch. I tried to sneak through the dining room and kitchen to the door to the basement without him seeing the pill bottles in my hand.

I went downstairs to the basement to find a place to hide and take the pills. I looked down at the pill bottles in my lap and started to cry. How had it gotten to this, I wondered? And at that moment, I saw no way out. That was the moment Kery came downstairs to argue again and found me crying and angrily asked what I was doing. I yelled back at him, "None of your business." That's when he saw the pill bottles I was trying to hide in my lap, and he asked if I had taken any of the pills. "What does that matter to you?" I said and then yelled at him, "Just go away!"

He wouldn't leave and tried to get the bottles away from me, and I fought him and held on to them and looked at him like he was crazy. What the heck did he care if I did this or not? It was obvious to me he didn't love me or want me, so why wouldn't he just leave me alone and let me do what I had to do? He stood his ground and ordered me to give him the bottles, and I said, "No, I'm obviously damaged goods, and you don't seem to like me, so just get out of my life and leave me alone."

But he still refused to leave. He stood there above me, looking down on me on the floor and said, "I'm not going to accept that as an excuse, not when you have a God that can heal you!" Then he left me alone in the basement with the pills still in my lap.

I sat there on the concrete floor with all the pill bottles in my lap, and I thought about what Kery had just said. I knew it was true. God could heal me. He could help me through this, and a tiny glimmer of hope opened my eyes.

I came to my senses and finally realized it wasn't about Kery; it was about me. I had to take care of myself, so I slowly got up.

Completely exhausted, I climbed the stairs and walked past Kery, who was standing in the kitchen. I went to the bedroom, shut the door, got into bed, and quietly cried myself to sleep. My heart was broken but at peace. I didn't realize it then, but I believe now that God used Kery to save my life that day.

The following is a song by Plumb called "Damaged." When I read the words to this song, they explain who I am to myself a little bit. I realized I was still that broken victim of my past, and I knew I had to give it up. I couldn't change the past or what happened, and God had even given me the strength to forgive my dad. But I was still living it.

"Damaged," a song by Plumb

Dreaming comes so easily
'Cause it's all that I've ever known
True love is a fairy tale
I'm damaged, so how would I know
I'm scared and I'm alone
I'm ashamed
and I need for you to know
I didn't say all the things that I wanted to say
and you can't take back what you've
taken away
'Cause I feel you, I feel you near me
I didn't say all the things that I wanted to say
and you can't take back what you've
taken away
'Cause I feel you, I feel you near me
Healing comes so painfully
and it chills to the bone
Will anyone get close to me?
I'm damaged, as I'm sure you know
There's mending for my soul
and ending to this fear
Forgiveness for a man who was stronger
I was just a little girl, but I can't go back

My friend Debbie from work knew what was going on with me and Kery. She tried to help by getting closer to us and invited me and Kery to go with her and her husband to the Idaho Falls baseball game. I figured it might help, so that night when I got home, I asked Kery if he wanted to go. He said he didn't know. We ate dinner in silence, and I got up to do the dishes. When I was ready to go, I went into the living room, and he was sitting on the couch watching television. I asked if he was going to go, and he just said indifferently, "No, I don't think so."

All hope for us drained out of me, and I was sick and tired of the silent treatment. For some reason, this incident was the final straw for me. I just lost it. I yelled at him, "Get out and don't be here when I get back! I hate you. Just get out of my life. I don't care if I ever see you again!" I stormed out the front door and slammed it as hard as I could and went to the baseball game with Debbie and Bill. When I got home that night, Kery was gone.

When I first realized he wasn't there, I was glad he was gone. I started envisioning my new life without him. Life was easier and more peaceful. I had no intention of ever getting back together with him.

I talked to his mom on a regular basis and cried my heart out to her. It was good to be able to talk to someone who knew Kery. She told me he was staying with his friends Marshall and Joanne. I figured that was perfect; he could get back with Kathy.

After things settled down and I was living without him for a while, the anger subsided, and I was able to think clearly. I was so disappointed that I was looking at yet another divorce. I wondered if I would ever have a decent marriage.

A little more time went by, and I realized I actually did not want Kery and me to get a divorce, but I didn't know how to fix us. I also didn't know if it was too late.

We had not talked at all since he left, and I wondered how he was feeling about me. I knew he didn't like me and was not ready to come back home. We did not speak for about four months, and I started praying to God and asking him to help me and tell me what I should do.

I remembered when Kery was home, every time we made up after a fight, I would tell him, "Kery, we need Jesus in our marriage,"

He would always just say, "Yeah right."

I didn't know if I was going to be able to convince him to accept Jesus, but I knew we wouldn't be able to make it without him. Kery was raised Mormon, and that had soured him on any kind of religion.

God Intervenes

It had been about six months of separation when I got really sick. It started out like flu symptoms, but I kept getting worse. I couldn't eat, and then I couldn't drink, not even a drop. Oz was about ten or eleven years old, and he tried his best to take care of me. Pretty soon, I couldn't even touch water to my lips without gagging. I was in bed and couldn't move, or I would throw up. I had never been this sick but didn't really know what was wrong with me, and I couldn't get up to go to the doctor.

Kery's mom had been calling to make sure I was all right, and when I had been sick for about a week, she called him and told him how sick I was and that he needed to get over to the house as soon as possible to take care of me. When he got there, I was unconscious. I don't remember him getting me out of the bed and into the car to go to the hospital emergency room.

Kery told me that when he got me to emergency, the doctors immediately put me on IVs to rehydrate my body. They must have done an ultrasound to find out that there was something going on inside of me that was causing the problem, and they were going to do emergency exploratory surgery to find out exactly what it was so they could see if they could fix it.

Later, when I woke up in the hospital bed, they told me I had almost died of dehydration, and the initial problem was caused because of my intestines. Intestines are free-flowing inside, and mine had adhered (grown) to the healing scar of my hysterectomy that I'd had a year prior. They were twisting around and around until my bodily systems came to a stop and was the reason I couldn't even drink a drop of water.

When I woke up after the surgery, Kery was there, and he stayed with me most of the time. In a few days, they allowed me to go home, and it was Kery who pushed the wheelchair out to the car and helped me get into the vehicle. We drove home in silence, neither of us knowing what to say or what to expect. I wondered if he would just take me home and leave me or wait until I was better, then leave.

I wanted him to stay, but I was afraid to ask because of the possible disappointment. When we got home, he helped me inside and told me to sit on the couch while he changed the sheets on the bed. Then he came into the living room and helped me get settled into bed, and I fell asleep immediately, worn out by the whole ordeal.

Peace and Love

Kery was bringing in food and water even though I wasn't eating much, and it took me a few days before I felt good enough to get out of bed. They had cut open my belly to do the surgery, and it was difficult to sit up. But I slowly got out of bed, trying not to hurt myself where the incision was, and slowly walked into the living room where Kery was sitting in silence.

It was early evening. The television was off, and there was only one lamp lighting the room. So it was quiet and calming. Kery was sitting on one end of the couch, and I sat down on the other end and got comfortable. He asked how I was doing, and I told him I was feeling a bit better and that I wouldn't be doing sit-ups for a while. I asked how he was doing, and he quietly said he was fine.

I had been thinking about what to say for days and wasn't sure how it would go. But I bravely asked him, "Well, what now? Tell me, what do you need to make you happy?"

He didn't hesitate and said, "I just want peace."

I paused and thought about what he said, and I realized right then that he was hurting, and he wasn't being arrogant. I felt sorry for the way I had treated him, and I realized that underneath that arrogance, he had emotions and feelings too.

"After all, he's just a man," said Tammy Wynette, and those words—"He's just a man"—made me realize he was human, and I felt so bad for all the heartache I had given him. We had fought about so many worthless things that didn't matter at all.

He then asked me what I needed to be happy, and I choked up as tears filled my eyes as I realized he might care. I said, "I just want to feel loved."

Again he didn't hesitate, and he looked at me with concern and sincerity and tenderly said he would do everything he could to show me he loved me. I, in turn, told him I would do whatever I had to do to bring peace to our home. I felt like we were making a major move to get back together, and he was obviously willing to try.

Then he moved down closer to me and took me into his arms, trying not to hurt my incision. We didn't speak. We just held each other quietly, and my heart surged with love and forgiveness for this man. We had failed each other and made such a mess of our lives, but now we were looking at a possible new start.

Sinner's Prayer

It was a couple of months before Kery and I had another little spat, and when I told him for the umpteenth time that we needed Jesus in our marriage, he said, "I think you're right." I stopped in my tracks.

I took advantage of the moment and said, "Well, I think we need to pray, and you can invite God into your life."

"What exactly does that mean?" he asked, and I told him the Bible says we are all sinners, and we need to repent of that sin and ask forgiveness.

"It's just a prayer—talking to God to ask him to forgive you," I said, and he said okay.

We went outside to the back porch and got down on our knees, and I told him just to repeat after me. "Dear Lord, today I come before you, and I admit that I am a sinner, and I am asking you to forgive my sins. I want you to be Lord of my life. I believe you died for my sins and that you were resurrected. Please forgive me for my sins against you. Amen."

We got up from our knees and hugged each other tight, and at that moment, I felt God knitting our hearts together. My heart was right next to Kery's rib that he symbolically gave to me, and we were becoming one. We both knew we were heading in a different direction together, finally.

We started attending church at the Christian Center in Idaho Falls and sat near the back, and one day two guys came up to us and introduced themselves. After church, we stayed to have doughnuts and coffee, and the two guys and their wives found us again. We found out they were Lynn and Brenda and Eric and Connie. We sat at a table and ate our doughnuts with a cup of coffee and talked.

When the guys started talking about bow hunting, that was what opened the door for Kery, Lynn, and Eric to become friends. Lynn and Erik had been Christians for quite a few years, and they took Kery under their wings and helped him grow in the Lord. They took him to the men's ministry meetings and to Promise Keepers so he could learn about God.

I'll never forget those days when Kery would come home from those events and cry as he would try to tell me about the speakers and how his heart was moved by what they said. I could see him changing before my eyes. The first time I saw Kery raising his hands to God in church during praise and worship, I cried. Tears streamed down my face as I raised my own hands to thank God.

He had done a major miracle for us through my sickness and trip to the hospital. It had forced Kery to come home and take care of me. God had orchestrated every bit of it to bring us back from that dark place to this new place of loving each other and loving God together.

We were at a new season in our lives, and I didn't want to mess it up again. So I decided to go see a Christian counselor for life advice and see if she could tell me how to be a better wife.

The counselor's name was Shanna, and we met once a week for quite a while. She helped me work out quite a few issues that seemed to be confusing to me and also gave me good advice about being more kind and forgiving. When we started talking about my mom, I told her about our mother-daughter history and her alcoholism. I told her I didn't remember Mom ever combing my hair or holding me and telling me she loved me. I told Shanna how difficult it was to even pick out a Mother's Day card each year for my mom. All the cards had endearing sayings on them, like "You're wonderful/giving/caring/unselfish," but I didn't remember her ever being wonderful, giving, caring, or unselfish. In fact, she was mainly selfish.

Then Shanna said one simple thing to me that changed everything. She said, "Patsy, you do realize you don't have to buy your mother a Mother's Day card?" This came as a great surprise and realization, just like the concept of forgiving my father had come. I had never thought of not getting her a Mother's Day card.

I thought it was a requirement. Shanna and I prayed together, and I forgave my mom. It was then that I really started healing from my past.

In the end, what I realized was that although it was my dad who did the worst damage and affected my life the most, it was Mom who also injured my heart by not protecting or defending me. She never beat me. She hardly even yelled, but she took my daddy's word over mine. It didn't matter to her what he had done to me. Also, even though he didn't mean to, Chip had actually abandoned me when he left that day. I was left all alone. My younger siblings didn't know or understand what was going on at the time, so I was left to fend for myself.

I can't explain why my dad did what he did to me, and I'll never know why. All I know is that I had to forgive him and my mom. Forgiveness really is the key to unlock the chains that bind us. Forgiveness sets us free.

The Bible says our enemy, the devil, just wants to steal, kill, and destroy us, and he almost accomplished destroying me. I came very close, but God saved me time and time again. All my life, he was there and deep inside; I knew it. Even when I was being abused, he was there protecting me from even worse, and he knew in the end I would survive and tell my story. Those days are over, but they are almost like a blessing to me because I have become a living testament of God's grace and glory. Sinful humans will act like sinful humans. That's no doubt, and it's proof that everyone needs Jesus.

> "For I know the plans I have for you," declares the LORD, "plans to prosper you and not to harm you, plans to give you hope and a future." (Jeremiah 29:11, NIV)

Many of us are damaged and hurting. We can live in anxiety and fear or struggle with depression. We can carry guilt and regret and end up using alcohol or drugs to cope. We can live with unresolved anger in our hearts and not know how to ask for help. I was physically and sexually abused, and I lived alone and isolated for many years. But I have also learned that with God, anything is possible—and anything is not "some things" or a "few things." *Anything* means *all*. With God, *all* things are possible. Matthew 19:26 says, "Humanly speaking, it is impossible, but with God everything is possible." He can heal our broken hearts, give us abundant life, make our life right, give us a hope and a future, and bring love and healing into our lives.

Today when I stop and think about my dad and mom, there is no hate. My memories take over for a minute, and I get these confusing heartfelt feelings of yearning for their love. But immediately, because I belong to Jesus, I am overcome by a peaceful feeling of him telling me, *Settle down. I love you, and that is all that matters.* In my mind, I almost run behind Jesus like a little girl would. Jesus knows I did the right thing by forgiving my father, and he knows I love my dad and my mom. But he knows I still have the memories, so he consoles me when I go to the past in my mind, and my heart and mind become clear again.

We just have to believe God's Word and take it all to heart because he is our only hope, the only one who has the power to truly heal our hearts. Once we believe in him and his Word, then we have to believe every promise he gives us, especially the ones that will help us heal.

It may seem out of reach, out of our understanding, out of what we ever knew, and it may seem hopeless, but we have to look to him and put our trust in him. He really does love us, and he gave us his love willingly by dying on the cross to prove he does love us. John 15:13 says, "There is no greater love, than to lay down one's life for one's friends." No greater love *ever*, and he loves you with this greater love. No man or woman can ever love you enough to save you, and no one would die on a cross for you, only Jesus.

Isaiah 53:5 (NIV) says, "But He was pierced for our transgressions, He was crushed for our iniquities; the punishment that brought us peace was on Him, and by his wounds we are healed." When our heart and mind are damaged and injured by others' words and actions, it is like we have big open wounds on our body. We can't help but focus on those wounds because they are open and oozing, and they hurt. We can put a Band-Aid on the wound, but it doesn't heal it. So we end up (like I did) focusing on our wounds until we can't see anything but our wounds.

But there is hope. The Word says "we are healed," and all we have to do is open our eyes and accept it. His Word and love is the healing salve that can heal our wounds, and it's the only thing that can and will heal these inner wounds. His Word is love, and that love can get inside our hearts and minds and clean out all those wounds. Then they start to heal, and once they heal, they become scars, and scars don't hurt.

Matthew 6:33 says we should "seek first His kingdom and His righteousness, and all these things will be given to you as well." The New Living Translation says it this way: "Seek the Kingdom of God above all else, and live righteously, and he will give you everything you need." It took me a while to figure out what this meant, and to me, it simply means to stay on the path he set out for us, and he will provide everything I need. When we get off that path, we can get beat up by the world. In his kingdom, he is the King, and he rules and reigns over us. He provides our food, shelter, and yes, our healing. We are in this world, but if we belong to him, we are not of this world. Because we have him, we have power and authority in this world.

Read your Bible, listen for his voice, ask him for advice. He does lead and help us, so be like a child with no fear and trust in him and love him with all your heart, mind, and strength. It's the first commandment! If we live "kingdom-minded," we can live this life expecting a miracle right at the perfect time, right when we need it. He is real, he is alive, he does live in us through his Holy Spirit, and he will never leave us or fail us. He will never abuse us. I have this vision in my head that I love to recall. I see me waking up in the morning, and I am in this huge princess bed that has a canopy of lace and twinkly lights. The bed is like lying on a cloud, and the covers are soft and featherlight. I get up and wash my face and brush my teeth. Then I go down to the dining room where there is a huge banquet table, and at the head of the table is God (who looks like Jesus), sitting on his throne. It is an amazing feeling to look at him on his throne. It is more than I can fathom. My heart is overwhelmed with love, and it is his love in my heart.

Proverbs 3:5–6 (NLT) says, "Trust in the Lord will all your heart; do not depend on your own understanding. Seek his will in all you do, and he will show you which path to take." I surrendered to him long ago, and I gave him permission to lead and guide my life. I don't want to depend on my own understanding any longer; it is flawed. But since I gave him permission to speak in my life, he leads and guides without me even asking. It just happens right in front of me. I see his hand in everything I do.

God made us for relationships—and he made relationships for us. He created us to be connected to him and to live our lives in community with others. But here is the thing: every time we're hurt deeply, we're faced with the option to let that wound define us and our future, or we can turn to God, who loves us and will never leave us or hurt us. He is someone we can trust.— Unexpected emotional wounding is so painful because that is what it is—unexpected.

How important for us then to understand that even when people leave us and hurt us, God never leaves us or forsakes us. He promises to be there for us and to help us. "The Lord is close to the brokenhearted, he rescues those whose spirits are crushed." People can be unfaithful, let us down, not keep their promises, but God is always faithful.

Trusting God is the fuel that makes our faith move forward and get stronger, and it is what made me who I am. I trusted my parents, and they failed me. I've trusted a lot of friends during that time, and they failed me. But when I learned to put my trust and faith in God, he never failed me. I was deeply wounded by the ones I trusted my life with, and it was difficult to release the clutch I had on the arrow that was piercing my heart and allow God to remove it. But I did, and he did, and I am finally free! Now I can let down my guard, knowing God has my back, and I have been able to make some amazing friends. It's wonderful what God can do with a broken and damaged girl like me. He is my everything.

Just like songs, scriptures have always spoken into my life and made me who I am. This is a prayer Hannah prayed that I have made my prayer because it is so true of my own life:

> Then Hannah prayed "My heart rejoices in the LORD! The LORD has made me strong. Now I have an answer for my enemies; I rejoice because you rescued me. No one is holy like the LORD! There is no one besides you; there is no Rock like our God!" (1 Samuel 2:1–2, NLT)

My story has been a journey, a lifetime of getting to know God, and I haven't arrived yet. We all have our own journey, and mine started before I was even born. It's was like having a godfather that knew my mom and dad and was very close to me and knew when she got pregnant. He was there when she gave birth and looked in the window at my tiny body and smiled. He was behind the scenes but was always there. He even traveled to the places we lived.

I remember when I started realizing he was there. I used to write him letters. He kept his eye on me. He was the one who talked to Wendy and Mr. Margiotta about my first job and apartment. Little by little, I realized there was someone who cared about me, following me. He knew I had been hurt and damaged by my parents, so he did his best to protect me from. He kept nudging me to keep on the path, but though I knew right from wrong, I always seemed to choose the wrong thing to do over and over. The good thing, though, he never gave up on me even though I didn't even give him the time of day! I even quit writing and calling. I had no time or desire to be with "grown-ups." I went about my business, failing at every step. I cried often, but I cried all alone. All the while, he was there with his shoulder and good advice.

He brought me the gift of love when I was twenty-seven, and it changed my entire life, past, present, and future.

I needed a miracle, and he came as a baby. My heart is so full of joy because of what he has done in my life. He healed me and made me a strong woman, and now I can say to my enemies, "You have no say in my life any longer!" He became my true God Father, and we have been together ever since. I love talking to him and spending time with him. He is my best friend.

I'm just so thankful he rescued and redeemed me. I am forever grateful. I know that when you realize just how much he loves you, it will bring light, healing, and love into your life. Seek him, and you will find him. He is waiting for your call.

Part 2—A Miracle-Filled Life

When you surrender your life to God, your life will change. You start to live with a purpose and a mission, not to mention joy, love, and peace. When God is leading you down the path he laid out for you, life is more abundant because he is walking with you. I won't say there are no troubles, but he is always there to walk you through any valley or over any mountain. He is ever present, and he loves and delights in us as his beloved children.

Just imagine—you are on a hike in the mountains. God gets you completely prepared for the hike. I like the thought of the intimacy of God walking with me. He loves me so deeply and knows my heart's longings and the hurts. He's exactly like a friend who is stronger and healthier than I am, so when he looks back and sees I am struggling, he comes back to help me. If I fall and scrape my knee, he sits me down on a log and gets out his healing pack and gently cleans the wound. "Does it hurt?" he asks softly.

"No, it's okay." Then he puts his hand over the wound, and when he lifts it, it's healed. I'm amazed. We start walking again, but now he walks by my side and helps me over the bigger rocks. At one time, he picks me up under my arms and lifts me up and over a bad mess of downed trees. As we are walking, he points to the top of a hill that is shining in the sun, and he says in a whisper, "That's where we are going." I look closer, and there are deer, elk, and wolves frolicking in the high meadow. *Strange*, I think, and he says, "I created them to get along."

Can he read my thoughts? I think, and he just smiles down at me.

I was driving down the road one day, and a thought came to me that I had not heard a particular song I liked on the radio for a very long time, and five minutes later, that song came on the radio. I knew it was him. It had to be, and I was moved to tears. Oh, how he loves us!

When I was a young believer, I used to keep a journal by my desk, and I would write my prayers and requests down each day. When a prayer request was answered, I went back and noted how God had answered. And soon my journal was full of answered prayers. It was a strong faith builder for me as I was getting to know my Daddy God.

I started my life as a towheaded little blonde girl playing on the beach, and I was full of dreams. But the dreams abruptly stopped when I was nine years old. And yes, I had a long, hard road out of that dreadful misery, but I know that God was with me and helped me every step of the way. Who knows what would have happened if he had not been there? Maybe Daddy would have succeeded in killing me. He set a new path before me that included him, and I try my best to stay on that path every day.

It may seem very strange, and it even seems that way to me. But those days of sexual and physical abuse have become a blessing to me. I say this because if I had not endured this hardship, I may not have the pure and abundant love of God in my heart as I do. See, I lived as a victim, and I didn't trust anyone. My fear was that they would hurt me the same way my dad did, so I lived in that fear. But the opposite of fear is trust, and finally being able to trust God enough to let go of the fear opens the door to receiving so much love from him that it leaks out in buckets! Oh, the joy, the freedom! It was the answer to my life's biggest question—*why*. Well, the answer to my big why was so I could learn forgiveness. Romans 8:28 says, "We know that God causes everything to work together for the good of those who love [and trust] God and are called according to his purpose" (NLT).

And if it hadn't happened, I definitely would not have this story to share that could be the very words that can help another victim of abuse. When my sister Pam died of cancer so young, a friend told me there was not just a reason for everything; there was a *good* reason. I have never forgotten that. God has a good reason for everything, and he does not mean evil for us. He makes everything good out of the bad. His love is supreme, and just his touch heals our hearts.

I don't want to live my life alienated from God. I want and need him to be in my life, and I want to stay on his path, so I start my day with him. The minute I wake up, I realize I am alive for another day. Corrie Ten Boom used to say a prayer every day, and I wrote it down on a pink sticky note and put it on my bathroom mirror. It says, "Good morning, dear Lord. This is your day. I am your child. Show me your way." I memorized it, so now I just say it when I wake up.

Then I get a cup of coffee and sit down to do my Bible study with my friends. We all have smartphones, and we downloaded an app called "YouVersion." The YouVersion app has the complete Bible in whichever translation you want, and it also has Bible study plans you can do alone, with a large group (like your local church), and with your friends. The plans are on practically every subject you can think of from marriage, motherhood, worship, reading through the Bible, and biblical study, just to name a few.

My girlfriends and I take turns picking the plans and sending it out to our group. The plans are usually five or seven days long. Each day includes a devotion, the scripture reference, then a place to type in your response to what you feel God is saying to you regarding the devotion. We have been doing these plans for a few years, and as we share our hearts, we become closer as we read and comment on one another's responses each day. I am in Idaho (or Baja), and my friends are in Arizona and Washington. It's a wonderful tool to use to keep us connected to God and close to one another.

I have a One Year Bible, and I read the daily scriptures that usually include a portion of the Old Testament, the New Testament, Psalms, and Proverbs.

I have an Amazon Alexa (because I love music), and I can ask Alexa to play "praise and worship" music, and I get some good music. I can also ask for "Bethel music," "Hillsong music.," or "instrumental worship." Much of the time, this is what I listen to all day. In my car, I have Sirius radio and channel 63 is the Message.

Staying on his path is a lifelong journey, and when you stay on that path, there is evidence of him in your life. When things start to unravel, you will know you took some sort of side channel or detour that didn't get you back to the main path.

My Life with Kery Secrist

Oz was nine and Jen was seventeen when Kery and I got married on April 11, 1987. We all moved into his little two-bedroom house on Eleventh Street in Idaho Falls.

This is one of the songs we played at our wedding, and though we had a couple of bumps, it finally did come to define our life together.

"Nothing's Gonna Stop Us Now," a song by Jefferson Starship

Looking in your eyes
I see a paradise
This world that I found
Is too good to be true

Standing' here beside you
Want so much to give you
This love in my heart
That I'm feeling' for you

Let 'em say we're crazy
I don't care 'bout that
Put your hand in my hand
Baby, don't ever look back

Let the world around us
Just fall apart
Baby, we can make it
If we're heart to heart

And we can build this dream together
Standing strong forever
Nothing's gonna stop us now
And if this world runs out of lovers
We'll still have each other

MY LOVING DADDY

Nothing's gonna stop us
Nothing's gonna stop us now

I'm so glad I found you
I'm not gonna lose you
Whatever it takes
I will stay here with you

Take it to the good times
See it through the bad times
Whatever it takes
Is what I'm gonna do

Let 'em say we're crazy
What do they know
Put your arms around me
Baby, don't ever let go

Let the world around us
Just fall apart
Baby, we can make it
If we're heart to heart

And we can build this dream together
Standing strong forever
Nothing's gonna stop us now
And if this world runs out of lovers
We'll still have each other
Nothing's gonna stop us
Nothing's gonna stop us

Oh, all that I need is you
All that I ever need
And all that I want to do
Is hold you forever, forever, and ever hey

And we can build this dream together
Standing strong forever
Nothing's gonna stop us now
And if this world runs out of lovers
We'll still have each other
Nothing's gonna stop us
Nothing's gonna stop us

We can build this dream together
Standing strong forever
Nothing's gonna stop us now

Cancer for Pam

My sister, Pam, called me from Florida in 1990 and said, "Patsy, I don't know what's wrong with me. I have been bleeding for about a month now, and it won't stop." I was immediately concerned and told her she needed to get to a doctor as soon as she could. She did, and they couldn't figure out what was wrong, so they decided to do a hysterectomy. When they opened her up, that is when they saw the damage of the cancer inside of her. They stopped the hysterectomy and told her she needed to be strong to fight the chemotherapy and radiation instead of the body working hard to heal from a hysterectomy. We were all devastated. Cancer was a killer, and at the time, we didn't know anything else to do but follow the doctor's orders.

They performed the radiation, and it was so hot it burned holes in her bowels. She had to have a colostomy bag hooked to her side. I felt so bad for her. Here she was, a beautiful young woman of thirty with a ten-year-old daughter, and she had this poop bag hooked to her side. It seemed so unfair to me, but she took it all in stride.

Colorado Miracles

For a short time, Mom was living in San Diego, California, with Steve and his wife, Annette. Annette was so good with Mom. She was just that sort of person, always patient and kind. Mom, on the other hand, was demanding and rude.

Mom's brother died and left her some money. It was about $50,000, and she came to believe that Steve and Annette were stealing her money. So she went to the bus station and caught a bus headed for Colorado Springs, Colorado.

Kery and I didn't know she was in Colorado Springs until we got a call from a bank there saying Mom was out of money in her checking account but was continuing to write checks on the account. We didn't have money to send and decided our only option was to go to Colorado Springs and bring her back to Idaho, where we could help take care of her. So we traveled to Colorado and rescued Mom. She was surprised and not happy to see us. We tried to explain the situation to her, and she balked but begrudgingly packed her suitcase. She sat in the back of the Oldsmobile and complained pretty much all the way to Idaho Falls. We got her into low-income housing in Idaho Falls; then we had to go back to Colorado Springs to empty out her apartment. We found out that much of Mom's stuff had been moved to a U-Haul place, so we gave them a call to find out how much she owed. They told us it was about $30.

Kery was working for Waters Building at the time, and we borrowed the old company truck, which had dual tires on the back. The truck had been sitting in the shop for years and had not been used, so we were a little concerned about it making the trip. We weren't rich and had exactly $150 to get to Colorado Springs, get Mom's stuff out of storage, and back to Idaho Falls. We put gas in the truck before we left and had $120 left.

We made it to Colorado Springs without any mishaps, and when we got there, it was quite easy to find the U-Haul facility. We went in to talk with the people. The girl at the counter gave us Mom's bill, which included a lot of late charges and totaled $90 instead of $30. We told the lady behind the counter we did not have the money to pay all those extra charges, and we thought it was only $30. She didn't want to budge, but finally after a little begging, she agreed to take off the late charges. We gave her $30 and had $90 left, and that was the first miracle.

We packed up the back of the truck, and the fridge was the first thing to go in. It was facing backward. We piled mattresses and boxes all around it in hopes the fridge would hold it all in because there was no tailgate on the truck. The rope was wrapped around the fridge a couple of times and then hooked to the sides of the truck bed. Kery tied a blue tarp around it to keep the mattresses and boxes dry if it happened to rain.

As soon as we gained speed, the blue tarp started to flap; but by then, we were on the busy freeway. With the blue tarp flapping wildly, we headed toward Denver and looked for an exit. As we traveled down the freeway and got closer to Denver, the traffic got thicker and slowed down to a crawl.

I was looking in the side mirror, and Kery was looking in the rear-view mirror. We both saw a long sleek black car coming up behind us. It was going fast, switching lanes like a fast motorcycle would do. It was getting closer and closer, and it didn't look like it was going to slow down. We watched as the car was right behind us, and then it looked like the driver was going to try to make it through the space between us and the car next to us. We both braced for the obvious impact because there was no way there was enough room between us for the black car to make it. But the next thing we knew, the black car with its blackened windows was past us. It was speeding ahead of us in the traffic like a black fish swerving left and right. We looked at each other with shock. That black car seemed to go right through us. It was amazing, and that was miracle number two.

The sun was going down, and it was getting late. We started looking for a place we could stay. We took the exit to the next little town: Cheyenne, Wyoming.

We drove to the first motel we could see, and Kery went inside and came back out shaking his head. It was $89 per night. There was no way we could stay there. We only had $90 left to get us home, and we hadn't bought gas yet.

Then I saw the sign at a motel down the road. The billboard was flashing "$19.99/night plus dinner and breakfast!" We looked at each other, and we could read each other's minds. *Really?* We drove down there, and it was true, so we checked in! Miracle number three—thank you Lord!

We had a great buffet dinner and a breakfast off the menu the next morning. Kery decided not to put the tarp back on because he didn't have enough rope to secure it down properly, and we figured that no matter what he did, it would flap. We filled up with gas and headed out. We had $25 left.

The fridge, which was holding everything up, was tilting to the back a little, and I kept looking back to make sure the load was staying secure. Since there was no tailgate on the back of this truck and everything was attached to the fridge, if it went, we would lose the entire load.

We were traveling at about seventy miles per hour down Interstate 80 heading west when the refrigerator was leaning so far back it started to worry me. I told Kery he had better stop and retie it. When he stopped, he went around the front of the truck. And as he walked around, he noticed the front right tire was flat as a pancake—the rim was resting on the pavement.

Kery came around to my window and said, "You're not going to believe this—that tire is flat as a pancake. It's a miracle we didn't wreck! What's weird is that if it had been a slow leak all this time, it would still be leaking. If it was a blowout, it would be flat, but we would have felt it and probably wrecked. You can't drive on three tires at seventy miles an hour." Kery and I were both flabbergasted at how God had protected us, and we believed he had actually made the refrigerator tilt backward so we would stop. There was just no other explanation, and that was miracle number four.

We didn't have a spare tire, so Kery realized his only option was to hitchhike back to the nearest town to get a tow truck, and it was a Sunday.

We were about fifty miles west of Cheyenne, and we had seen signs all along the freeway saying "Do Not Pick Up Hitchhikers!" And we had also heard that criminals were hijacking semitrucks. In addition, the vehicles had to come up over a pretty steep hill and then down before they would see someone standing on the side of the road, so it wasn't a very good place to hitchhike from because most vehicles were going pretty fast down the hill, and it would be difficult to stop, especially the semis.

It wasn't very likely that Kery would get picked up, but he crossed the highway and got to the other side of the freeway going east and stuck out his thumb.

Most of the vehicles just zoomed by him, but it had only been fifteen minutes when a semitruck came up over the hill. He must have seen Kery immediately because you could see and hear the truck slowing down. Kery looked over at me, and I could barely see him smile toward me. I was so thankful someone stopped, and I watched Kery jump in, and they drove away. It was really a miracle someone could even stop for him and did, so this was miracle number five on this trip!

I had been sitting there in the passenger's seat of the truck for about thirty minutes when an older car passed by our truck. The car slowed down. My heart started to thump in fear as I watched the driver get out of the car and walk to the back and lean against the trunk. He crossed his arms and just stared at me. I knew he wasn't close enough to see my eyes, so I stared back. I was afraid he was going to start walking my way, but then he stood up, got back in the driver's seat, and drove away.

About ten minutes later, a police car pulled over right in front of me, and he got out of his car and walked to the passenger side of the truck. I rolled the window down.

"Are you okay? Do you need any help?" he asked.

I told him I was okay and explained our flat-tire situation and then told him about the car that stopped in front of me. He told me he would keep cruising by and keep an eye out for me, and I told him thank-you and immediately felt better.

It was another hour or so before a tow truck came rolling up with Kery sitting shotgun, and I was such a happy girl to see him. They hooked up the truck, and Kery and I both squeezed into the front seat with the driver. We drove back to Cheyenne.

The tow-truck driver was the only one there that day, and he and Kery worked for almost an hour to get the old rusted wheel off the truck; then they had to get the tire off the rim. The guy told us he wasn't sure if he had the tube we needed in stock because it was pretty obsolete, but he went to the back of the store to check.

As Kery and I sat there waiting for him to come back, we noticed a sign above the checkout counter that said "Labor—$45 per hour." Kery and I looked at each other, and our eyes said, *Oh crap*. We both knew he had just spent no less than an hour just to get the tire and rim separated, and he had also driven out fifty miles to tow our vehicle to his shop.

He came from the back of his shop and said, "You are not going to believe this! I found the tube for your tire! It was tucked away in the back, but it was there, and I found it!"

We were amazed that he actually found one! I called that one miracle number six!

He got the new tube put into the tire, got it filled with air, tested for leaks, and then put it back on the truck, and we were ready to go.

He got his receipt book out, and we braced ourselves for a big bill. He wrote "Tire tube, $5," and handed us the bill. We looked at it and almost started crying. We asked him if he was sure that was correct, and before we could say anything more, he said, "Yeah, $5 is all it is." That was miracle number seven for us. We thanked him generously and drove away.

As we were driving away, we were silent, just taking in the glory of God and how much he loves and cares for us. I had a scripture going through my head, and I got out my Bible and looked up Psalm 121 (NLT) and read it aloud to Kery.

I lift up my eyes to the mountains
where does my help come from?

My help comes from the Lord,
the Maker of heaven and earth.
He will not let your foot slip—
he who watches over you will not slumber;
indeed, he who watches over Israel
will neither slumber nor sleep.
The Lord watches over you—
the Lord is your shade at your right hand;
the sun will not harm you by day,
nor the moon by night.
The Lord will keep you from all harm—
he will watch over your life;
the Lord will watch over your coming and going
both now and forevermore.

I put in the one praise and worship CD we had, and worship music filled the truck bed. Kery and I sang along to the words at the top of our voices, praising the Lord our God from our spirits. Then it started to sprinkle rain, and a beautiful rainbow showed up in the sky right in front of us. Wow, we were just speechless. A sign from heaven itself was saying, "I love you, and I will always take care of you. Trust me!" How much better could it be? O Lord, thank you for miracle number nine.

We were almost home. We had about three more hours to go, and that's when we could see we were heading right into a storm. The mattresses and boxes were not covered, and we prayed we could get home before the storm hit. Well, the storm hit us about sixty miles from Idaho Falls, and it rained steadily the entire way home.

When we got to Idaho Falls, Kery pulled the truck right into the shop at his workplace, and we left it there for the night. We got into our car and drove home completely exhausted. The next morning, we went to check the load, and we couldn't believe it. Everything was dry as a bone. It had rained hard on us for more than an hour, but everything, even the cardboard boxes, were completely dry. We had ten undeniable faith-building miracles on this trip.

We eventually moved my mom to the Good Samaritan nursing home, and they loved her and took care of her, and she was doing well there.

Death of Chip

My sister, Pam, got progressively worse with the cancer and chemo. When she was too sick to function alone, she and Natasha moved to San Diego and lived with our brother Steve and his family. Annette took care of Pam, and we visited quite often, especially when she was having procedures done.

In 1992, I flew down to San Diego to be with Pam because we weren't sure there was time to drive. We thought we were going to lose her. Annette and Natasha (who was about twelve at this time) met me at the airport, and as we drove to their house, they told me all about Pam's current situation. She wasn't doing well.

As soon as we got to the house, everyone disappeared for a minute, and I was standing in the kitchen alone when the phone rang. I listened to it ring a few times, and when no one answered it, I answered it. It was my daughter, Jen, calling from New York. The first thing she said was, "Mom?"

I recognized her voice and said, "Jen?"

She acknowledged it was her. After the initial shock of hearing her voice, she asked me, "Mom, have they told you yet?"

"Told me what?" I asked.

"Oh no, Mom, I'm not going to be the one to tell you."

That's when I demanded she tell me what she was talking about. "Jennifer Michelle, tell me what?" And there was silence.

"Mom, you're not going to believe this."

By now, I was getting angry. "Jen, just tell me what is going on."

After a few seconds of hesitation, she told me, "Mom, your brother Chip is dead."

189

I dropped the phone, and my heart dropped to my stomach at the same time as I tried to grasp that Chip was dead.

Steve and Annette, their kids Dennis and Jessica, and Natasha all came in, and we got into a big group hug and cried together.

It has been earlier that Kery and I drove to San Diego to see Steve, Annette, and Pam, and we also planned on going to see Chip in Los Angeles.

Chip had been dishonorably discharged from the army because of drug use, and he ended up living in alcohol and drug rehabilitation homes most of his life. He would do so well in the system that he earned outside time. But not a month would go by, and he was back in full-time again. It was a sad, addictive circle he was stuck in.

We went to his rehabilitation home to visit him, and the whole situation just broke my heart. His room was bare: just a bed, a dresser, and a nightstand. The dresser had a TV on it, and the nightstand had a lamp and a Bible on it. I felt so sorry for him. He didn't have a wife and never had kids, so he was completely alone.

We found out that Chip was getting a welfare check each month that helped him get his personal items. This day, he got his check; but instead of personal items, he bought drugs. He went back to his "home" high on cocaine and alcohol, and he got there after 10:00 p.m. when they lock the doors. He stood outside banging on the doors, begging them to let him in, but they ignored him and called the police. The police came, and because he wasn't really breaking the law, they took him to the nearest hospital. The hospital put him into a straitjacket, shot him up with something to calm him down, and then put him in a dark room. They left him for the night, and when they went back the next morning, he was dead.

We found out later that when you give that particular medication to someone who is obviously on some kind of high (like cocaine), you have to check their vitals every half hour. And this hospital did not check on him even once during the night.

A reporter from the *Los Angeles Times* was doing an undercover investigation of this very thing because it was happening quite often at that hospital. She contacted us later, urging us to sue the hospital for wrongful death. My brother Steve actually contacted an attorney about this, and we found out about wrongful death suits. The death has to have life-changing hardship on, first, his wife, then his children, or finally his parents, in that order.

Chip did not have a wife or children, and Daddy was dead, and Mom—well, we had just recently had Chip's funeral in Los Angeles. There was only me, Kery, Jen, Oz, Steve, Annette, Dennis, Jessica, Natasha, and Mom at Chip's funeral service. Mom was sitting there in the chapel, and out of the blue, she said loudly, "What the hell are we doing here? He deserved to die!"

We all reacted with shock and looked at her and wondered how she could say something like that about her firstborn child, but that was Mom.

The good news, though, when Jesus came into my life, I wrote a letter to both my brothers and my sister, telling them about Jesus and how they absolutely had to give their lives to him. It was Chip who wrote back and told me I had lost reality, and I was crazy. But one of the rehabilitation homes he was in was called Christ's Crusaders, and then it was Chip who was sending me pamphlets and long letters about accepting Jesus.

Death of Pam

It was a little over a year later in the spring of 1993 that Annette called to say that Pam had passed away peacefully, listening to the music of Bread on the stereo.

I remembered that a few months before she died, she pulled me to her bedside and told me not to worry, that she had read the book I had sent to her about Jesus, and she had accepted Jesus into her life. We had smiled at each other. She had brown doe eyes and long curly dirty-blonde hair, just like mine. It hurt my heart that she had to live with this cancer, and I knew one day it would kill her. And sure enough, it did. I didn't get to see her again. She was thirty-three years old when she died.

Now two of my siblings were dead, and both were because of the effects of our upbringing. I talked to Pam's doctor about the cancer she had, and he told me that the cancer had started in her cervix. He told me that cervical cancer sometimes can be caused by early sexual activity. Chip was addicted to drugs and alcohol most of his adult life. Both deaths caused by the dysfunction of our family.

Steve and Annette Move to Idaho

After Chip and Pam died, Steve was my only sibling, and I begged him to move his family to Idaho where we could all be closer. They packed up and moved to Idaho the next summer when school was out. Steve, Annette, Dennis, Jessica, and Natasha found a house near us and moved in. They began going to our church. It was like heaven having my own brother sitting next to me at church.

We spent quite a bit of time with them. We had them over for dinner, and we went to their place. We were all so happy to be together again. I used to go over to visit Annette, and we would sit at the kitchen table and talk for hours. I loved my little red-headed spitfire sister-in-law. She made me laugh, and she always amazed me.

Annette studied to become a certified nurse's aide, and later she worked in a home for retarded adults. She took her shift feeding them, changing them, bathing them, and keeping them company. It takes a special person to be able to do that, and Annette was that person. She was my hero, and I just thought the world of her.

Steve was a tool- and diemaker, and he flew to different jobs around the country to make the tools they needed for building the space shuttles and F-16 fighter planes. He was very smart and had worked his way up to this level of work. And I was proud of him.

Natasha got pregnant when she was sixteen years old. Annette and I talked her into giving the baby up for an open adoption. I knew a lady from church who facilitated Christian open adoptions, and she knew of some people who were looking for a baby boy.

Annette and I went to meet up with my friend and find out more about open adoption, and what we found out was just perfect.

The family adopting the baby would keep in touch with the mother of the child as long as she was interested.

Natasha didn't want to give up her baby, but she knew she was young and had no way of supporting a baby. Knowing she could keep in touch with the adoption family, she finally agreed to meet with my friend and find out more. And the next step was to contact the new family.

Bruce and Sherry came to Idaho Falls from California to pick up their new baby. Natasha had named him Adrian Robert Ward. They were very happy to meet Natasha, and they fell in love with the baby. It was time for them to go, and we cried and held each other. Bruce and Sherry sent us all letters and pictures on numerous occasions, and they renamed the baby Mitchell Adrian. He was well taken care of and had a loving family, and we all felt at peace.

Then one day, while Steve was gone out of town working, Annette just disappeared. I called and went to her house a dozen times, to no avail, and I was beginning to worry about her and the kids.

Kery and I played on a softball team for our church, and after the games, we went to a local burger and shakes hangout called Arctic Circle. One of Jessica's friends and her mom were in the Arctic Circle that night, and they came over to our table.

"Did you hear about Annette?"

Kery and I looked at each other, then looked at her. "No, we haven't. As a matter of fact, we have been trying to find her."

"Well," she said, "Annette has been selling methamphetamines to the neighborhood. She has taken the kids out of school, and they are doing the drugs too."

Kery and I were shocked and didn't know what to say. The next day, Kery and I went to her house one more time, and this time, we just went in when she didn't answer. The mess we saw was beyond belief. Dishes were piled up in the sink and both counters and looked like they had not done dishes for a month. Next to the washer was a huge pile of dirty clothes. It looked like they had gone through all the clothes in the house and never washed any. There were empty beer and Coke cans and pizza boxes all over the house on the floors, and there were needles and spoons all over the place too. The carpets were torn up and stained terribly. The mattresses were all pulled off the beds, and the bathrooms were black and filthy. We walked around looking at the house and couldn't believe what we were seeing. It was so bad we didn't want to touch anything.

We went home, and I called my brother right away. I begged him to come home. "You need to get home immediately." I told him I had heard Annette was on drugs and that she had taken the kids out of school, and she was selling drugs to the neighborhood.

He listened and said he would come home right away. We met him at the airport and took him straight to the house. We all went in and walked through the house, and Steve was just as stunned and puzzled as we were.

Before we left the house, we all made the decision to call the police. I picked up some of the needles and spoons and put them in a plastic baggie (for evidence) and put that into my purse. When the detectives got to our house, we told them everything we knew, and I remembered the plastic baggie I had in my purse and ran to get it. I brought my purse back to the table and brought out the plastic bag, and the detective looked at me like I was crazy. Then he said, "You know, if you had been stopped by the police and they found this stuff in your purse, you would have been in a lot of trouble!"

I told him it wasn't mine, and he said, "That's what they all say!"

They finally found Annette and put her in jail, but they couldn't find the kids. Steve went over to the house and finally found Dennis, but Jessica had run away, and Natasha was nowhere to be found. Steve didn't hang around. He and Dennis headed for Texas where they had lived before, and he asked us to keep our eyes open for Jessica. A few days later, we found Jessica at the house, but she ran. We had to chase her down. We took her immediately to the airport, and even though she didn't want to go, we put her on the next plane to Texas.

Annette ended up at the Pocatello Women's Prison, and we went to visit her often. She was sentenced for six years for forgery of checks she had stolen to buy her drugs. She was doing well in prison and even gained about twenty pound while she was in there. She said she was reading her Bible, and just as importantly, she was clean.

She went back to court, and the judge told her if she could keep clean for one full year, they would take off the other five years. But she had to find some decent people to live with, so she called us. We trusted her and wanted to help, so we willingly opened our house to her and told her she was more than welcome to come live with us and that we would try our best to help her have a better life.

She arrived at our house on a Sunday. On Wednesday after I got home from work, she asked to borrow my car. I let her, and she didn't come back. Later that week, she called to apologize and said she had left my car down the street with the keys in it, too embarrassed to face us. Then on Friday, when we were at work, she and Natasha went to our house and stole much of my jewelry, including Mom's rings and Jen's little gold turquoise ring with the tiny *J* on it that Bruce and I had given her, as well as our movie camera and a couple of other things.

We called the police, and they picked up Annette and put her back in prison. And Natasha disappeared again. I was devastated by the whole experience and went to the local jewelry stores to see if I could find my cherished jewelry. I didn't care about the movie camera or anything else they stole from us, but the rings and jewelry they stole were priceless to me. Luckily for me, I found a few pieces at the closest jewelry stores, but sadly, Natasha's name was on the receipt as the seller.

Annette spent the next five years in Pocatello Women's Prison, and while she was in prison, Steve divorced her and married a lady in Texas named Rhonda. But they only stayed married for a very short time.

Death of Mom

After Steve had been in Texas for about a year, he called and told us he missed Mom and asked if we would fly Mom to Texas to live near him. Rhonda found a good place for her to stay and got her signed up. We took her out of the Idaho Falls Good Samaritan Center, and I took her to the Salt Lake City airport. She was elderly, so we were able to get a wheelchair for her. The airport bellboy had to take her through security, so we put her on the elevator.

I watched my mom as she was rolled into the elevator, and I told her I loved her. But she didn't say anything to me. I knew it would be the last time I would see her alive, and it was. She died less than a year later. Kery and I didn't go to the funeral, but my brother Steve and I did fly to Elk Park, North Carolina, to bury her in her family plot.

Steve and Rhonda only stayed married for a couple of years. I only met her once when she and Steve came to Tetonia, Idaho, where Kery's family had a cabin. It was wintertime, and we spent the weekend in the cabin and played in the snow.

Annette got out of prison five years later and went to Texas to stay with Steve, and Natasha somehow ended up in Texas too. But after a short time, both of them ended up back in prison there. Today, as I write, Annette and her daughter Jessica are both in prison in Texas.

Sydney Paige Piantes—First Granddaughter (March 23, 1997)

When Jen was almost eighteen, she shocked us all by joining the army and was placed with the 101st Airborne Division. She ended up in Kuwait fighting a war but came home alive.

Jen got married to Curt, and they moved to Saratoga Springs, New York. When they had been married a year or so, she found out she was pregnant. She sent me her ultrasound picture in a Federal Express package. She gave us her due date and insisted we get our tickets as soon as we could because she was afraid the time would come, and we would not be able to afford the trip to New York.

So we got our tickets to go to New York nine months in advance and at an amazing price of $44 each roundtrip! On March 22, we drove to Salt Lake City, Utah, and got a motel so we could catch our early flight. On March 23, we woke up in the motel and called Jen's house. There was a message on their machine from Curt that said, "Hi, Jen is in labor, and we are at the hospital."

We thought for sure we would miss the birth of our first grandchild. It would take all day to get to the Albany, New York, airport, and we had layovers in Denver, Colorado, and in Atlanta, Georgia, and we worried all day long.

Finally, we landed, and Jen's friends came to pick us up, and we rushed down to the hospital. And we were so happy to see she still hadn't given birth. It was about 8:00 p.m. by the time we got there, and Sydney Paige was born just a couple of hours later. Talk about perfect timing! She came out white and blue, and the doctors put her in a warm incubator, and then they suctioned and rubbed her little body until the blood started flowing. Another miracle—we got there in perfect timing, and we had our first granddaughter.

Kery and I instantly fell in love with that tiny baby girl we called peanut. The next morning, we went to get some food, and Kery told me that he hoped Jen would allow him to be grandpa to that baby, and I told him, "Oh, honey, of course she'll let you. You are my husband, and you are her grandpa." Kery never had children of his own. He had been married before me for a very short time, and she had talked him into getting a vasectomy—his greatest regret. When we got back to the hospital, I told Jen what Kery had said. Jen took her baby and handed her to Kery and said, "Here, go to your grandpa." And that's all it took. The bonding was immediate, and what Jen did for my husband was the greatest gift he ever received, being called *grandpa*.

Today as I write, Sydney is twenty-two years old and graduated from the University of Oregon in June 2019. She is a smart and beautiful child. We are so proud of that little peanut!

Jen and Sydney

My Daredevil Son, Oz

Because we wanted Oz to have some stability after his dad and I divorced, we wanted him to grow up in one house and have the same friends through high school, so we stayed in the Eleventh Street house until Oz graduated and was ready to move out. In 1996, he graduated from high school and moved into an apartment with a friend.

Oz was a daredevil, so he was always getting hurt. He had no fear and just kept going. From the time he was about twelve, he has been pushing it to the limit. It all started with rollerblading, then snowboarding, skydiving, then base jumping off cliffs, and then he became a little safer when he got his pilot's license and started flying planes. He also did some mountain climbing.

He has broken most of the bones in his body including his back three times.

All I can say at this point is that he is going to be one sore boy when he is my age.

It wasn't long before he came to me and told me he had gotten a girl he was dating pregnant. He didn't know what to do, but I told him he had to marry her for the sake of the baby. We didn't want a little girl in this world who thought her daddy didn't want her. So they got married when Syringa was about five months pregnant.

Heather Kennedy Wilcox—Second Granddaughter (September 8, 2001)

On September 8, 2001, Syringa gave birth to our second grand-daughter, Heather Kennedy Wilcox. We called her Kenna. She was born a tiny baby, weighing in at less than six pounds, at the Eastern Idaho Regional Medical Center. We went in to see and hold her, and she felt so small in our arms. We felt like we were holding a little weightless doll. Kenna was a little blonde girl, just like her mom and dad and grandma. And when she was about one year old, Oz and Syringa moved them all to Boise. Syringa wanted Oz to move away from the friends he grew up with, thinking that might help their relationship, but it didn't really help much.

Oz worked as a painter and a cabinetmaker and tried to keep money coming in. Then one day, he was talking to a friend who said, "Oz, I think I am going to go back to school. I've decided to be a doctor. Do you know how much doctors make, dude?"

That got Oz thinking. *Hmm, I could use that kind of money.* He decided to go back to school and went to Boise State University to become Dr. Oz.

He started taking classes in the medical field, and before the year was over, he told me, "Mom, I hate this. I don't really want to be a doctor." He was taking DNA and laboratory classes and was not happy. His background was in construction. His dad was a talented carpenter, and so was Kery, so he changed to construction management, and that fit him like a glove! He had to pay for his first year because of his bad grades in high school, but that kept him in school; and after the first year, he was able to get student loans. He was on the dean's list his first year and went to school for almost six years because he couldn't go full-time since he had a family to support. He was in poverty the entire time he went to school.

Right after he started school, Syringa divorced him, and child support made him even broker. But he stuck with the school.

Unfortunately, with them divorced and not getting along, we were not able to see Kenna as often as we wanted to. Syringa would not tell us where they lived and threatened Oz that if he told us where they lived, she would take away visiting privileges. We fought against that, and in the end, Syringa didn't let us see Kenna because she accused us of not caring enough to come see her!

Kenna is now eighteen years old and is a beautiful girl. We hope to rekindle a relationship with her once she gets out on her own.

While Oz was still attending Boise State, he invited us to go to a football game to watch the Boise State Broncos play. I wasn't all that thrilled, but we went to Boise and got the blue-and-orange sweatshirts so we would fit in. We watched the Broncos for the first time, and they were very fun to watch. They won that first game we went to. Oz told us the channels on TV that would cover their games, so we started watching the games and really got hooked. We have gone to games there in Boise, and it is so fun to see them play on their blue field!

When Oz was close to graduating, he met Olivia. He told me once he couldn't have a girlfriend while going to school because he didn't have the time to devote to a relationship, but when Olivia entered the picture, that rule changed a little

Olivia impressed us as being a very sweet girl, and we fell in love with her right away. She was the perfect match for Oz. She liked how wild and independent he was and allowed him to do his own thing. She was open and friendly, and she seemed to like us. She was an outdoorsy kind of girl, and they did a lot of fun stuff together. They were happy, and I was happy for them.

Oz came to Kery one day and said, "I want you to marry us."

Of course, Kery told him, "I can't marry you. I'm not a minister." But Oz had done his homework and told him he could get ordained online, and that was good enough for him. So Kery got online and found out how to do it and became an ordained minister.

Oz graduated from Boise State University with a bachelor of science degree in construction management one week, and the next week, they got married.

I found a wonderful description of marriage in my Life Application Bible, and we worked up some good words for Kery to say over them. Oz and Olivia had their own vows to read too. It was a beautiful wedding and a beautiful day in Boise, Idaho.

New House—Rigby, Idaho

Once Oz moved out, we were "empty nesters." We decided to build a house a few miles outside of Rigby, Idaho. We started building in May, and it took us a year to build the house because we only worked on it weekends and evenings. We lived in our Idaho Falls house and went up to Rigby in the evenings and on weekends. In September, we decided we might want to put the Eleventh Street house up for sale because it isn't easy to sell a house in the dead of winter. We got a realtor, put it on the market, and it sold in four days—a full-price offer. We were surprised it sold so fast. This only gave us a few weeks to figure out what we were going to do. We ended up buying a trailer we could live in until the house was ready to move into.

It was about December when we had guys come in to do the sheetrock work. One day we came home from work, and our trailer was completely without electricity and was frozen. We found out that one of the guys doing the sheetrock had unplugged our power to plug in the power he needed. He did not realize the electric cord he unplugged was to our camper.

We went to church and were talking to some of our friends about our situation. We thought we would just move into Kery's mom's house, but a friend at church needed someone to house-sit his house for a few months—just the amount of time we needed before we could move into our own house!

In May, we moved into our beautiful house. Kery had done a wonderful job of building our house. It was like a big piece of furniture he had built by hand.

Idaho Winter Miracle

We almost died one cold stormy Sunday morning going to church. Our church was in Idaho Falls, and we had to travel on a highway into town. This particular day, it was snowing heavily, and there were snowdrifts everywhere. The highway to town was a complete white-out, which just means the wind is blowing the snow sideways. As we traveled, cars were playing it safe and going pretty slow. It was too slow for Kery, so he started passing them, going about twenty-five miles per hour in the left lane. All the cars were kicking up snow, and with the whiteout, we didn't see that there was a snowplow a few cars in front of us in the left lane, which was probably kicking up even more snow.

The snowplow was in the left lane to use the emergency turn-around so he could go the other direction, and he was going slow. We were going faster than the snowplow, and all of a sudden, there it was in front of us. Kery had to react fast. He knew better than to slam the breaks on because our car would have slid right into the back of the snowplow and caused a major accident there on the freeway. As I screamed, Kery made the quick decision to go around the snowplow on the far left, which meant we had to leave the highway, going about twenty-five miles per hour, and drive down into the borrow ditch and then up to the middle of the emergency turnaround in front of the snowplow and back into the borrow ditch on the other side, then back to the highway. The whole time, the car was rocking and rolling like we were on heavy seas. The driver in the big snowplow must have seen us and saw what we were doing and slowed down a little so we could pass right in front of him and get back on the highway. It took about ten seconds—and all of this in a whiteout, icy roads with other vehicles, and the snowplow. We didn't know if there was a car in the left lane or not. How we survived was a miracle, and we were both quite shaken. I felt like I was going to throw up. I don't know how Kery was still driving and didn't know how in the world our car didn't hit another vehicle. I started crying out of sheer fear and relief of what had just happened, and Kery just grabbed my hand. We started thanking God for saving us; then we sat in silence as he drove the rest of the way to church. We were both lost for words.

When we got to church, we walked in, and our friends noticed how shaken we looked. We told them what just happened, and they were as amazed as we were that we were still alive. I started crying again, and they hugged us, giving us comfort as they prayed for us and thanked God once again for how he had saved us.

Christian Music in Southeast Idaho—K-Love Radio

Southeast Idaho is predominately Mormon, so it wasn't surprising that there wasn't a Christian radio station available. We depended on our CDs and cassette tapes for Christian music.

Then one day, I pulled into the garage of our house; and as I reached up to grab something off the dash, I accidently hit the tuning dial, and the station went fuzzy. I turned the dial to reset the station when, all of a sudden, I recognized a Christian song playing. I thought it was just a fluke and waited for it to be over to see what was next. Then I heard the announcers talking about the new satellite station called K-Love, and it was broadcasting Christian music in our local area. I sat there in my car listening and crying and thanking God for this huge blessing of having a Christian radio station.

Jack's Death

Kery's dad, Jim, left their family when Kery was about ten years old. A few years later, Kery's mom, Carma (whom I lovingly call mom), married Jack. Jack Meisinger was a guy from Chicago, Illinois, who came to Idaho and fell in love with Mom.

Kery's mom and dad had three children of their own. Her sister died of cancer, and she had two young boys: Randall and Jared. Their father was in the navy and had no way of taking care of the boys, so Mom adopted them as her own.

Jack was a single man when he married Mom. He willingly took on her three teenagers and adopted her sister's two kids; then they had one of their own. He was a great dad to all six of them for about twenty-five years.

Then out of the blue, Jack had a heart attack. He was only sixty years old and had just retired from the Idaho Transportation Department. The night it happened, his natural daughter Michelle just happened to be visiting from Utah. Michelle called us on the phone and woke us, and we jumped out of bed and got to Mom's house as fast as we could.

When we got there, Mom and Kery's sister, Debbie (who lived next door), were trying to do CPR on him. He was lying on his back on the kitchen floor. When the EMTs arrived, they tried to resuscitate for a few minutes then loaded him into the ambulance to take him to the hospital.

We all got into cars and followed them into town to the hospital, and they put him on a respirator. They thought Jack might have a better chance of surviving with the technology found in Salt Lake City, Utah, so we followed them down to Salt Lake. But after a day or so, the doctors did a brain scan and found there had been no brain activity for too long, and that meant it was over. It was then that we as a family decided to let him go. It was the hardest thing to do ever.

Jack loved to fish, and God gave us the gift of taking him fishing a week before he died. We were supposed to take Debbie fishing, but she was sick that morning. So we went next door to Mom and Jack's house and asked Jack if he would like to go with us. He said yes, so we took him out on our drift boat to float down the south fork of the Snake River, and he had a wonderful day fishing all day long, not knowing he would be dead in a week.

My father-in-law was one of the finest men I had ever met. He loved his wife, and even though he wasn't a Mormon like she was, he went with her to attend the functions the church had. He protected her like a lion protecting her cubs, and he took care of her and gave himself completely to her. It took me about ten years to talk about Jack after he died without crying, and I was just his daughter-in-law. I respected, loved, and admired that man like no other. I miss him to this day, and I know without a doubt that Mom would be so much better off if he was still here with her.

Island Park, Idaho

Kery's family had a nice cabin in Tetonia, Idaho, that we went to often. Kery and his family, including his grandpa, built the cabin when the kids were younger. Mom and Jack went up quite often, and Mom spent her time painting the beautiful scenery around her, including the great view of the Grand Teton mountains she had. They had some good times at the cabin growing up, but when Jack passed away, Mom really didn't want to go up to the cabin anymore. She ended up selling it for enough money to buy a house in St. George, Utah.

In May of 2005, Kery and I bought a cabin in Island Park, Idaho. The town of Island Park is in the same caldera as Yellowstone National Park, which is only thirty miles away. Island Park gets an average of almost eight feet of snow each year, so it is a snowmobiling mecca in the winter.

The cabin we bought was an awesome place in an area called Buffalo River Estates. The lazy Buffalo River runs nearby, and thick evergreens kept almost every cabin naturally hidden from the road. Our cabin was an old mobile home that had a big bump out in the living room. It had two bedrooms, one on each side, and two bathrooms, with a dining room right off the kitchen, and a large living room and a bar. It had a woodstove in it. There was a snow roof over the entire trailer, and it covered a full deck on the front as well. We loved the cabin and fixed it up the way we liked it, and we went up almost every weekend all year long.

In the winters, we went snowmobiling most of the day, then snuggled in at night to watch movies, read books, and cook awesome dinners. Kery made a path from the front driveway to the side of the deck so we could drive our snowmobiles up onto the deck and then ride them right off the front porch onto the path and up to the front driveway. It took thirty minutes to ride the path where the old railroad tracks were in Island Park to the town of West Yellowstone outside of Yellowstone National Park and have lunch, and we did that often. We had four-wheelers for the summers, and we rode around on the same trails we rode on our snowmobiles.

Theft of My Identity—Natasha Diann

Natasha Diann, my niece, got out of prison in Texas and moved back to Idaho. She had just spent the last six years of her life in prison for check forgery (to buy drugs). She contacted me on a Saturday evening, and I was happy and surprised to hear from her. I invited her to come to church on Sunday to see Kery and me, and she agreed.

Sunday came, and church had started, but Natasha wasn't there. I wondered if she would even show up, but then it wasn't too long before she and her four young children showed up. Her oldest was about nine at the time, and the youngest was about four. They sat behind us, all five of them, and I couldn't help but turn around and just look at those beautiful, innocent children of my own blood. They all looked at me too, knowing I was Aunt Patsy, but not knowing who I was at all. My heart just kept saying to me, *We have some fixing to do, fixing relationships.*

After church, we took them to a local restaurant and bought all of them breakfast, making sure they ordered anything they wanted. Natasha told us what was going on with her. She was living with her in-laws, and she didn't have a job, and her vehicle did not have a working transmission in it.

We took deep breaths and knew we had to take the chance of trusting her. We told her we would do what we could to help her. We also told her we really wanted to have a relationship with her but explained it was hard to trust her. We hoped she would understand. She assured us she was different now and would behave better, so we gave her a couple of twenty-dollar bills and said goodbye and told her we would be in touch.

Kery started asking around for a used transmission he could get installed cheaply and found a few.

We decided to go up to Island Park to the cabin the next weekend, so I called Natasha and asked if she and her kids would like to go. She told me they would all love to go. The weekend came, and we went to Natasha's in-laws' house there in Rexburg where she was living to pick them up. We loaded their stuff into the back of our vehicle and headed up to Island Park, which was about an hour away. We chatted on the way and caught up with what was going on with us. It was good to spend time with Natasha.

We got to the cabin, and the kids were loving it. They were amazed and happy to be at our cabin in Island Park. It is absolutely beautiful there, with crisp, clean mountain air. We had our two four-wheelers up there, and the kids rode them all day long. They had so much fun. We took them down by the river, and they played in the chilly water, splashing and laughing.

That night, we made hamburgers and salad together and had s'mores around the fire for dessert. It was a great Idaho day. The next day, we headed home, and we dropped off Natasha and the kids at her in-laws. They all hugged us closely and told us they loved going. We had bonded with the kids, and they knew they had a great-aunt and great-uncle in Kery and me. They told us, "Thank you for such a fun weekend," and begged us to take them again, which we agreed to do. We loved the kids, and we were all happy we were reunited.

The very next week, I got a call from a credit reporting agency, asking me for more information about a credit card I had supposedly applied for. I told the woman on the phone that I had not applied for a credit card, and she was as confused as I was. She asked my full name, and I told her; then she asked for my Social Security number. Then she asked if my address was a street in Rexburg, Idaho, and that was when I realized what was going on. The address was Natasha's address. I recognized it because it was the same one she gave me to pick her up when we went to the cabin. I told the lady on the phone I knew the address, that it was my niece's.

While she was on the phone, she said she could look to see if any other accounts or inquiries had been added to my record, and unfortunately, there were more. Natasha had opened accounts at Victoria's Secret, Macy's, and a few others using my name and Social Security number. I told the lady thank-you and hung up.

I thought back on when and how Natasha could have gotten my information and then realized exactly what had happened. It was when we had all gone to the cabin. When we go to the cabin, my habit was to always leave my purse hanging over one of the chairs in the dining room. When we went to bed, my purse was right there, and she obviously took advantage of the situation. All she needed was my Social Security number to open any accounts she wanted.

I called Natasha and told her I knew what she had done. I told her she just needed to return everything she bought, and I would forgive her. But she denied doing it. So I told her I would give her exactly thirty days to return everything she had bought, and if she cleared all those accounts to a zero balance, I would forgive her and forget it.

I let it go for two weeks and then called on the accounts, and they still had a balance, which meant she had not returned anything yet. I found out she had ordered everything online, so she would have to pack up and return the merchandise by mail. I called her again and told her she only had two weeks left.

I was so upset she had done this, not because of the crime but because she needed me, and I wanted to help her, but she messed up again and showed us she couldn't be trusted. It hurt me that I was losing this relationship with her and those precious kids.

At the end of the week, I called on the accounts, and they still had a balance. So Kery and I went to the police station and told a detective what had happened. He listened to our story and then went to his computer to log the report and turned around with a surprised look and said, "There is already a warrant out for her arrest!"

We were shocked. "What else has she done?"

Well, we found out that she had been working at a construction company in and had stolen their company checks and had been writing checks all over town. So the construction company filed a report on her, and they had the warrant out for her arrest.

The police found her, and she went to prison again. And this time, she spent ten years.

Today, as I write, Natasha, just got out of prison in Idaho and is living in Idaho. I'm hoping to rebuild a relationship with her when we return to Idaho.

La Ventana, Baja California Sur, Mexico

Kery's dad invited us to visit him and his wife Sandie in La Ventana, Baja California Sur (BCS), Mexico, numerous times over the years, but we were a little hesitant to go to Mexico. We had heard about drug cartels and kidnappings, and it didn't sound like anything I wanted to do. Plus, we didn't know what we needed as far as documentation to go to Mexico. We finally gave in and applied for our passports. We flew into San Jose Del Cabo, and Dad and Sandie were there to greet us after we went through customs. We were there for two weeks, and that first week, Dad and Sandie showed us around the tip of the peninsula. We went to the Pacific side to go out on Magdalena Bay to see the big gray whales who migrate from Alaska to have their babies in the warm waters of Mexico. Todos Santos is a charming little town on the Pacific Ocean side with lots of shops and restaurants. Los Barriles is also a quaint little town that is right on the Sea of Cortez. We fell in love with the area. The people were kind and giving, and we felt welcome there. It was a paradise, and we asked Dad if we could buy property there, and he was happy to say *yes*! The second week we were there, we were looking at properties that were for sale.

After a few tries, we finally found a lot we liked and paid $11,000 for a little more than half an acre of cactus-covered land with a great view of the Sea of Cortez.

La Ventana is a small fishing village on the Sea of Cortez in a cove. It is about one hundred miles north of Cabo San Lucas and only thirty miles south of La Paz. About twenty years ago, it became a very popular kiteboarding destination because of the breezes that come from the north almost every day around 11:00 a.m.

Since 2005, when we bought our property in Baja, we have gone down for a two- to three-week vacation every year. Through the years, we have had a fence built around the property. We put in a large underground water container to provide water for showering, doing dishes, and watering plants. And we had electricity brought to our property.

In 2017, we had a small house built. It is an adorable little house that is only five hundred square feet. It has a combination living room/dining room/kitchen, one bedroom, and one bathroom. It also had a five-hundred-square-foot patio and a five-hundred-square-foot roof patio. We have landscaped the yard with native palm trees and cactus.

Baja is a beautiful paradise, and there is so much unique to this area. One thing unique to La Ventana is the beautiful island of Cerralvo, which is about twelve miles out. The waters are turquoise blue, and in the summer, they are warm, which makes the fishing great. The sun sets over the mountains and puts a pink hue on Cerralvo Island. The sun rises over the Sea of Cortez, and we have seen some of the most beautiful sunrises in our lives.

Goodbye to Dennis Charles Ward

In July 2007, the trout flies were hatching on the South Fork in Idaho, so Kery and I were on our way to go fishing. We had stopped at the store to fill up with gas and get some ice when I got a phone call from my brother. He was very distraught, crying and trying to talk, and I could barely understand what he was saying. He finally got out that his son Dennis and his friend had been floating the Trinity River there in Texas the previous day when their rubber raft had gone over a diversion dam, and it flipped over when it went over the dam. Both boys fell overboard and went under. Dennis got stuck in the swirling undertow and couldn't get out. His friend popped up a little way down the river, but Dennis did not. After a couple of days, they still hadn't found Dennis's body. Steve had been hoping Dennis had possibly just gotten separated from his friend and that they would find him alive downriver. The police had an all-out search for him and found nothing. A week later, they found Dennis's body about fifty miles downriver. Dennis was twenty-three, had a wife, two little boys and another on the way when he died on that river. Another loss for the Ward family.

Miracle Cousins

A week or so before Thanksgiving, I was at work and was visiting with my friend Sharon about Thanksgiving. She was telling me about Thanksgiving with her family. She said it would be held at her parents' house as usual and that all her siblings, their spouses, and kids would be there, both sets of grandparents and all her aunts, uncles, and cousins. She said they were expecting over fifty people. I was in awe of her very large albeit Mormon family

I went back to my desk and thought about my own Thanksgiving and figured if I were to have my own family over for Thanksgiving, it would be around ten people. My heart yearned to have a big happy family with cousins, grandpas, and grandmas, but I knew I never would. I never knew the love of a grandma or a grandpa. I met my grandfather on my dad's side one time for about an hour of my life and never even met a grandma. In fact, I didn't even know who they were, but God heard my hurting heart that day. And he had a plan he was setting into place for me.

It was only a few months later on a Sunday in March when we got home from the cabin. There was a message on our message machine that said, "Hi, my name is Karen Queen, and if your mother is Elsie Dunn, then I am your cousin! Here is my number. Give me a call."

I ran outside and told Kery, "Honey, come inside, listen to this voice mail. I have cousins!" And I started crying.

Kery was happy for me, hugged me, and said, "Well, go call her back!"

I called the number she had left, and a woman answered the phone. "Hello?"

"Is this Karen?" I asked, and when she said yes, I told her how happy I was to hear from her. She told me all about her family. We talked for an hour, and I found out she had a brother named Bobby, two more sisters, Joyce and Carolyn, and they had spouses, children with spouses, and even grandchildren. I was totally amazed. It was like one of those gift boxes you open that has another box in it and another box in it, until you get to a tiny box that has the best gift in it.

After I got over the shock of all this new "family," I told Karen we had just gotten home from Island Park where our cabin was, and she said, "That's so odd. We are just heading to Island Park, Ohio, to go to a Christian concert."

"Island Park?" I asked her. "To see a Christian concert?" I was amazed already, but this was heartwarming news. "Karen, are you a Christian?"

"Yes!" she said, and I almost started crying. What a blessing to find cousins who were like-minded and not atheists who would hate me for being a Christian.

I asked her one last question, "Do you listen to K-Love radio?"

"Yes, I do," she said excitedly.

I told her, "Oh my gosh, Karen, do you realize we are listening to the same music at the same time?"

"Yes, I know that!"

We were both so excited to find each other. She told me that one of her sisters had my phone number years ago but was too shy to call, thinking I would reject her for some reason. I guess you never know "who" they will be or "how" they will react to your call. I think I would have had a hard time too.

Then purely out of curiosity, not expecting the answer she gave me, I asked her what church she attended, and of course, she said "A Nazarene church." And that's the church we were attending in Idaho Falls, Idaho. It was all just too amazing. She was a gift from God to me. She was family, and she wasn't just a cousin. She was a sister in Christ too.

In October of that same year, Kery and I flew to Ohio to meet and visit my newly found cousins, and every single one of them met us at the airport. There were about thirty of them. I had never felt so loved and accepted. We cried together and just wanted to stay as close as we could to one another so we didn't lose one another again.

We had a few all-family dinners, and on our last night, we all went to Applebee's for dinner, and my cousin Joyce's five-year-old granddaughter Aubrey came up to me as we were getting ready to say our goodbyes, and she looked up at me and said in her little-girl voice, "Welcome to the fam-i-ly."

Tears came to my eyes, and I got on my knees and gave her a hug and told her, "Thank you, Aubrey." How precious the words that come from the mouths of babies. Since then, Karen and her husband, Kevin, have come to visit us in Idaho. And we have been back to Ohio again. All of them are my miracle cousins because God loves me and gave me a family.

Moving Out of Idaho

Kery had his own business as a building contractor, and he always had a custom house to build. I was still working at the Idaho National Lab. Together we were keeping our heads above water, and we were doing okay.

He had about six guys working for him most of the time, and they built quite a few houses in the area. I thought he worked too hard. He came home every night beat up, tired, dirty, and had been pounding nails all day. I told him he needed to spend more time drumming up business instead of working in the heat and cold, but that was who he was. He worked alongside his guys, and they appreciated it. If they were late, he docked their pay; and even though most of them were not believers, they started each day with prayer, as directed by Kery. I was so proud of him. His guys respected him, and he did a good job.

Destruction of a Construction Company

A building developer came to Idaho Falls from Utah. His name was Dave, and he wanted to build a few upper-end houses on the Rigby Golf Course, in Rigby, Idaho. Kery found out about this opportunity and made a bid to build. Dave interviewed a few guys and decided on Kery. So he and his guys began working on the first house, and it was turning out beautiful.

They were finishing up the first and began working on the second house at the same time. This house was different but turning out just as nice as the first. About halfway through the second house, Dave disappeared and stopped paying Kery. Kery could not find him. Kery sent his draw requests via Federal Express, but Dave never sent him his money. This went on for months, and Kery was having to use his own money to pay his guys and the subcontractors. When that money ran out, Kery had to stop work on the house.

When Kery stopped work, that was when Dave showed up and was going to file a complaint against Kery for stopping work on this second house, and they were at a standstill. Kery had no intention of finishing the second house if Dave was not going to pay him. Kery realized this was much deeper than the stop work. Kery finally had to get an attorney to try to recover the money Dave owed him for the work he and his subcontractors had already done. The attorney went to bat for Kery because it was evident Dave was in the wrong.

It finally went before a judge, who could understand Kery's case, but the judge ruled that Dave had committed fraud. But it was fraud against the bank first because, legally, the draws were taken out of the bank with the sole purpose to pay the contractor (Kery) for his work, and Dave was drawing it out and keeping it for himself. So

Kery was put in second place and received no money. So Kery was left with nothing. It was a shame that the judge ruled that way, but it was the legal position.

Dave claimed bankruptcy, and so did the bank. Kery was left with all the attorney's fees, as well as the money owed to all the subcontractors, plus his own guys. It totaled around $200,000. Many of the contactors knew Kery and knew he was a good man who had tried to get their money, so they wrote off the debt. The other contractors did not know Kery from Adam and wanted their money immediately. Unfortunately, this all happened during the big 2008 mortgage and housing crisis, and banks were not lending money. So no one was building, selling, or buying houses. Builders who had built "spec" houses were going bankrupt because no one could buy their houses. It was a bad time for everyone in the building business and for anyone who wanted to buy or sell a house. In the end, we were left with about $150,000 in debt, and it all went on our credit report as unpaid judgments.

Kery tried to keep our head above water. He did a lot of remodels and repairs, and luckily, I was still working for the Idaho National Lab. We were able to tread water, but it was difficult because Kery's income was our major contributor.

We tried to figure out a way out of our debt, and I came up with the idea to update both of our résumés and send them to my former boss Kathy, who had moved to Tri-Cities, Washington. She was working for one of the subcontractors at the Hanford Site. This was a long shot, but we were willing to take whatever we could get.

Kery and I discussed the issue of sending Kathy our résumés. There were a couple of dilemmas—the first being, could and would Kery, the Idaho-born and bred man, move out of Idaho? I suppose he secretly hoped Kathy wouldn't call with a job for either of us because he had no intention of leaving his beloved Idaho.

Our second dilemma was, if she found a job for me first, how would I move to Tri-Cities alone and start a new job and find a home etc. without him there? How could I move to a completely foreign city by myself, and how could we afford to put me up and feed me separately? It didn't seem possible for our situation, so we really needed Kery to get a job there first.

But God

"For I know the plans I have for you," declares the LORD, "plans to prosper you and not to harm you, plans to give you hope and a future." (Jeremiah 29:11, New International Version)

One day in June 2009, Kery got a phone call from a manager at Hanford, where Kathy, my former boss, worked. The caller was a construction manager who was hiring a carpenter. For a month or two, he had gone through over four hundred job applications, and he finally found the guy he wanted to hire, but the guy he chose did not pass his background check. So the construction manager was back to square one and was very frustrated.

This construction manager was in Kathy's office telling her this story and told her how frustrated he was. Kathy listened patiently then reached into her drawer and pulled out Kery's résumé and handed it to the construction manager and simply said, "How about this guy?"

The construction manager read over the résumé and asked Kathy if she knew this person, and Kathy told him, "Yes, his wife was my secretary, and Kery has done work for me in Idaho."

The manager took out his cell phone and called Kery. When Kery answered, the manager introduced himself and told him Kathy had given him his résumé. Then he asked Kery, "Are you willing to move to Washington State?"

Kery hesitated and then said, "Well, I think so."

The construction manager said he had a meeting to go to but would call him in the morning.

Kery told me about the phone call, and we talked it over and prayed about it. We realized this could be God providing a job for us.

The next day, the construction manager called Kery and again asked, "Are you willing to move to Washington State?"

This time, Kery said yes, and the construction manager said great and told Kery he would have human resources write up an offer and get it to him.

Kery was shocked that it was so easy. Normally, you don't get your foot in the door at a federal government job without a background check and a medical exam, which takes months to set up and complete. We both knew it was a God thing. Only God could get an Idaho boy out of Idaho and into a federal government job in Washington with a phone call.

Kery moved to Washington and lived in our tent trailer while I stayed in Idaho and packed up the house. He came home every other weekend when he had a Friday off to help me pack up. When we finally got the house packed up, we rented a U-Haul truck and hauled it all to Richland, Washington. Kery had already rented us a house in a neighborhood called Bird Hill in West Richland, Washington.

One of our first weekends in that house was July 4, and we didn't know where to go to watch the fireworks, so we stayed home. But we found we really didn't need to go anywhere—the whole neighborhood was lighting up fireworks of their own, and we had quite a show.

Soon after we arrived, we began searching for a home church and went to four or five before we found Columbia Foursquare Church in Richland. It was a medium-sized church that was Spirit-filled and had great worship music. We immediately knew God wanted us going to this church. Our spirits felt at home there as it was similar to the Nazarene Church we had just left in Idaho Falls. Pastor Jon and Candy were the first to come to us after the service and introduced themselves, then invited us to breakfast. This was the beginning of a great friendship.

Candy told me about a Bible study some ladies were doing called SOAP and invited me to attend. We met at the Starbucks coffee near our house. SOAP is an acronym for *scripture, observation,*

Application, and *Prayer*. Five or six women usually showed up. Candy would give us a scripture to look up, and we would read it together. Then we would write down the scripture and what we *O* (observed) the Word was saying. Then we would write down how we could *A* (apply) that Word to our lives. Then we wrote down our *P* (prayer) for God to help us apply this Word to our life. When we were done writing, we would each share our SOAP. We would share our hearts, and there was so much healing and love going on. The insight we got into one another's lives was priceless. We all became very close friends.

After a year or so of doing this together, Candy took on another responsibility and asked if I would mind leading the ladies SOAP study. I told her I would but also explained, "I am not a leader!"

I took over for Candy, and we girls kept on going with our SOAPing. It ended up that for the entire nine years we lived in Tri-Cities, Washington, I attended and lead the ladies' SOAP. Some of the girls would come and go, but there were some of us who were together the longest, and we became very good friends.

Every six months, the church put on ladies' and men's "encounters" at a beautiful home on the river that had about six bedrooms. It was rented out for these kinds of purposes. Women from the church invited their unchurched kids and friends. The women who were leaders at the church would each take a topic and spend about an hour speaking about that topic. There was an average of eight women who needed Jesus that attended. It was a very impactful weekend, and many of the unchurched came to understand Jesus a little better and ended up surrendering to him.

Candy asked me to be one of the speakers and to speak on forgiveness. She said, "I don't know anyone who knows God loves them more than you do. Your story of forgiving your dad is so powerful!" I was very timid and hesitant about accepting. I told her I didn't think I could do it, that I was too shy to speak in front of all those women. She assured me I could do it, so I reluctantly accepted.

I arrived about thirty minutes before it was time to speak. I had notes the church had given me and added my own notes for my talk. I was very nervous but was bound and determined to do this. Candy was counting on me. The attendee girls sat around on the couches and chairs in the living room, and the speaker had a podium near the fireplace. I noticed that some of the speakers sat off to the side behind the couches at some round tables.

I saw Candy, and she saw my nervousness and gave me a hug and said, "You will be fine." Then it was my turn to speak.

I got up, and the first thing I said was that I was not a speaker or a leader, but I did have a story of forgiveness to share. I started telling my story, and all the girls listened closely; some had tears rolling down their faces. I looked over at Candy, and she just smiled and nodded her head, as if to say, *You are doing fine.* It was difficult for me to talk about the sexual and physical abuse from my dad out loud to a group of people. I was emotional and even had to stop periodically because I was choking up and couldn't talk. Then I started telling them about the goodness of God—how he had loved me enough to rescue me, teach me about forgiveness, and then heal my heart.

When I was done, many of the girls got up and gave me a hug, and I felt very understood. Some of them told me they had suffered similar things, and they appreciated me telling my story. It had helped them. I didn't like being the center of attention, so I sat down on the couch. Candy came up behind me and told me quietly that I couldn't sit there. The living-room area was for the attendees. I jumped up, feeling very self-conscious and uncomfortable. I realized that the leaders who were sitting at the round tables were probably thinking what a stupid I was. I moved around to the back of the couch, around the round tables, to the door in the back of the room. The next speaker had started, and I felt desperate and alone. I went out to my car, started it up, and went home.

Normally, the leaders were there for the entire weekend but something had happened to me. I felt completely out of place and didn't feel like I belonged. I was not a leader, I was not an attendee, I was me, and it wasn't enough. No one even knew I had left, but Sunday at church, some of the attendees came up to me and asked where I had gone. They told me they had looked for me so they could talk to me. I felt horrible. What was wrong with me?

There was so much good about where we were. I got a job pretty quickly, so we both had good jobs that paid well. We had a nice little house, and we had found a great church. The weather was awesomely warm compared to Idaho, and there were Christian churches on every block. It was a breath of fresh air, and we were quite a few hours closer to our kids too.

The house Kery found had white Berber carpets, and in the backyard was a huge walnut tree that had no grass under it, only wet dirt. Each day, the sprinklers came on and wet down that dirt, and it became mud again. And Sadie, our five-year-old chocolate Labrador retriever, loved to run around in the backyard and the mud. Of course, she came in through the doggie door and brought all that mud into the house on her feet, right onto the white carpet. I ended up vacuuming every night after it had dried. Kery had signed a year's lease, so we couldn't move for a year. At least the mud part was just during the summer.

When we were getting close to the year being up, we started looking for a different place, and it turned out it was quite difficult to find a place that would accept dogs (we had two shih tzus and Sadie). There were probably thirty houses for rent, and maybe five of them accepted animals. The rentals that were pet friendly were quickly gone way before we even had a chance to call. We had to vacate the house before the next month was out, and we were having no luck, so we prayed and talked it out and remembered that we had planned on living in a trailer or fifth wheel down in Baja. We thought we might as well buy it now, live in it, and get it paid off; and when we were ready, we would take it down to Baja. So we started looking for a trailer.

Fifth-Wheel Miracle

We really wanted a fifth wheel, mainly for me. A fifth wheel is easier to pull than a trailer because it is attached to the bed of the truck. But we only had our Tahoe and couldn't see buying a new truck just so we could pull a fifth wheel, so we started to look for a trailer. Kery looked in the paper for used trailers, and the first one we saw was pretty cheap and was on a used-car lot. From the outside, it didn't look too awful bad, but the inside was torn up, and the previous owner was obviously a smoker. There were brown nicotine stains dripping from all the walls, and it stunk like an ashtray. We couldn't get out of there fast enough.

Then we drove over to the new RV lot and looked at some of the RVs to get an idea of what we wanted. We saw some pretty nice ones but knew we did not want to pay $45,000 for a trailer. All we had was about $20,000 in my 401(k), so we started looking on Craigslist and the ThriftyNickel where we found quite a few.

I generally got home a little while before Kery did, so I was on the computer looking on Craigslist and found an ad for a fifth wheel that came with a truck. I read the ad again, and it was being sold by a Christian couple who just wanted to get out of debt.

The description of the fifth wheel and the truck sounded perfect to me, but even though I knew Kery would more than likely approve of the fifth wheel, he had to like the make, year, and style of the truck too. I called him at work and told him about the deal I found and asked if he would drive a Dodge truck and gave him the description. He said he might, and we decided we would go look at it as soon as he got home.

231

As we were driving over there, we prayed and asked God for two things: one, that we could afford the price of the truck and fifth wheel; and two, that we would both be in agreement about buying this fifth wheel and the truck, if it was the right thing. There is nothing worse than when Kery wants to buy something major, and I don't agree; or if I want to make a major purchase, and he disagrees. We wanted to be united about this decision.

When we pulled up to the house, there was a beautiful red truck parked on the street, and Kery couldn't help but wonder if that was the truck that went with the fifth wheel. We got out of the car, and the owners met us midyard, and the man started walking Kery and me toward the beautiful red truck and opened the door. The inside of the truck was immaculate, and we were both impressed. He told Kery to jump in, and they could take it for a spin to get some gas.

While they were gone getting gas, the lady and I went into the backyard to where the fifth wheel was parked, and she unlocked the door and opened it up. I went up the steps and stepped into the living room, and it was so immaculate and nice I just about fainted. I loved the layout. It was perfect for us. The kitchen was at one end instead of in the middle like a lot of them are, and the dining room and living room were both part of a bump out that made the living room bigger. Then you go up two stairs to a bathroom, with a good size shower on the left and a sink and mirror on your right, as well as closets. The "bedroom" had cabinets above the bed and on each side.

Kery and the owner came back from getting gas and approached the fifth wheel, and they checked out the outside first. He was showing Kery all the storage compartments and that they were all full of ropes, chairs, and tools. He was letting it all go with the fifth wheel. Then Kery went inside and liked it just as much as I did, and we walked around the outside for a few minutes and then walked slowly to the front yard. I could see Kery thinking real hard about it. It was exactly what we were looking for, but how much did they want for it?

Kery asked him how much, and he told us seventeen thousand for both the fifth wheel and the truck. He explained that he and his wife were Christian, and they just felt the Lord telling them it was time to get out of debt. We were almost shocked, and Kery looked at me and said, "What do you think?"

I immediately told him, "I'm ready to sign on the dotted line!"

Kery said, "Okay, you have a deal."

The couple were elated, and so were we. They got out of debt, and we got a new home. All four of us stood on their driveway with tears in our eyes, and because we were all Christians, we held hands and thanked God for the blessing of the deal. It was perfect, and we knew this was another gift from God.

We would be able to move out of the rental house the following month, so we gave our notice. We had to start looking for a place to park our new fifth wheel. Kery called the Horn Rapids RV Resort. They said they were full but would put our name on a waiting list, and it could be a while.

We drove over there to see what kind of place it was and went inside the little store to introduce ourselves. After we had talked a few minutes to the lady behind the desk, she said, "You guys seem like really good people. I think we have a place available that you would like."

We were surprised and thanked her, and she took us around the park and gave us a couple of options. We chose the back row against the farmer's field. After we put all of our stuff into storage, we moved into the Horn Rapids RV Resort.

Fifth-Wheel Living

It took some time to get used to fifth-wheel living, but the fifth wheel we were living in was perfect for us and easy to live in. We had everything in storage, and our boxes were numbered. I had a spreadsheet with a list of what was in each numbered box, so it was easy to go get something we needed. The only drawback was it was difficult to have people over because the inside was so small for more than us, but we didn't often have that many guests.

Horn Rapids had a swimming pool and hot tub and a small store where they carried basic food, batteries, paper plates, etc. Our parking spot was on the back row so we could easily leave our place and take the dogs for walks on the dirt road.

Thanksgiving Day 2011

In 2011 on Thanksgiving Day, my younger brother Steve was giving his grandsons motorcycle rides around the block, and no one had helmets on. They were going around the block slowly, and no one knows exactly what happened. But the motorcycle hit some gravel, and it threw the motorcycle on its side. Steve went flying. Ethan, one of his three grandsons, was on the back of the motorcycle and was seat-belted on the back. Steve had broken ribs which punctured his lungs, and he had slammed his head into the graveled road, which knocked him out. They called an ambulance and Steve, was admitted into the hospital, and this was where the trouble began. He was a smoker and a drinker, so when he didn't have either, his body started going through withdrawals, which caused more pain, especially on his broken ribs. So the doctors put him into an induced coma so they could control his pain. After about a month or so, they took him out of the induced coma, but he would not wake up on his own and ended up in a coma. I was in contact with the hospital on a daily basis, and they were keeping me well informed of Steve's condition.

After he did not wake up for a couple of weeks, Kery and I decided to go down to Texas to see if we could help wake him up.

Steve's friends Don and Jeanie met us at the airport and took us to their house for the first night. They were both so kind and generous, and we appreciated them greatly. The next day, Don took Kery and me to Steve's house, and we got settled there. Don waited while we put our bags into the house, then took us to the hospital to see Steve.

Steve's eyes were closed, and he had a breathing tube down his throat. They had to use a respirator because Steve was not breathing on his own. We talked to him, and I really believed he might hear us. We had heard that people in comas can hear someone talking to them, and we hoped it was true.

The nurses told us that sometimes when they turned Steve's body over to change the sheets, his eyes would open. They asked if I wanted to be in there when they turned him over, and I said yes, I would. They closed the curtain, and it took both nurses to turn him over using the sheet. They were on one side of the bed, and I was on the other, and I was talking to Steve the whole time, watching his eyes. And when they turned him, he did open his eyes, and tears came out of his eyes for the first time.

One of the nurses noticed and said, "Oh, look, a tear! He can hear you!" I started telling him to wake up and told him I loved him. I told him what had happened to him and that he was just in a coma, and everything was going to be okay. When they were finished, they turned him onto this back again.

The nurse told me they had not seen any tears up to this point, and it was obvious he was reacting to me being there. I was so moved, so happy, so ecstatically charged that I left his bedside and went to Kery, where I burst into tears and sobbed against his chest. I couldn't believe how relieved I was, that I knew he was going to be okay. I had been so scared I was going to lose him.

After a week of being there, we went back home feeling better, and I continued to stay in touch with the hospital and his friends, who cared very much about him. The hospital would only talk to me about his condition, so I called each morning and sent a text to everyone after each call every day. Steve finally opened his eyes, and they took the ventilator out, and then he had to go to physical therapy for a while.

After a few months, Steve tried to go back to work at Lockheed, but the injury to his brain had altered his thinking. And he had mood swings and would talk irrationally. He was harmless, but he was scaring people.

Lockheed offered Steve a disability retirement, but he argued with them that he was not disabled. They tried to bring him back again, and it just didn't work. He got a job driving semitrucks, and he got into two different jams. So they let him go. He couldn't find a job he could keep because of his injury. He finally had to sell his motorcycle and his house because he couldn't afford to keep them. He wasn't his normal self, and we had tried to help him. He ended up in the veterans hospital for evaluation, and they determined that he did indeed need some mental help. He has lived in their homeless shelters since they admitted him.

A judge finally legally described Steve as disabled, and he has started to receive Social Security Disability and received a huge SSD check retroactive to when he first lost his job. He is doing better but is still not the old Steve.

Briar Dawn Wilcox—Third Granddaughter (May 30, 2012)

May 30, 2012, the day our third granddaughter, Briar, came into the world. It was too easy, and it happened fast. Oz called us in the morning to let us know Olivia was in labor and was at the hospital, so we got dressed quickly and went down to the hospital. Olivia's parents, Blaine and Jana, were in the room with Oz and Olivia. Olivia seemed rested and happy when we got there and didn't seem uncomfortable at all. She was sitting up in bed, chatting with all of us. After we had been there about a half hour, we decided to go get coffee. So we left and headed down the street. Before we got one mile, Oz called us and said, "We have a baby!"

We were shocked! We ran back to the hospital, and there she was, a tiny, little blonde-haired girl. And her name was Briar Dawn Wilcox. Dawn is Olivia's middle name. She was tiny, and when I held her, she was warm and snuggly and just lay there peacefully in my arms. *What a miracle*, I thought once again.

Very soon after she was born, Oz took a job that sent them to Western Washington, but we made a lot of trips that way to watch our newest little granddaughter grow up. They were living in Silverdale, Washington, and they came to visit once in a while.

Red Mountain House

We lived in our fifth wheel for about three and a half years, and during that time, we learned how to live in a small place. We also got all our debts paid off from the Idaho real estate disaster. It was a blessing to live so cheaply for those years, but after that amount of time, we just started feeling like we needed to find a more permanent place. Kery was missing being able to tinker in a garage or work in the yard or build something, so we started thinking about moving into a house again.

We contacted a local real estate agent, and one morning we met him at a coffeehouse and sat down to talk about what we were looking for. We were looking for three bedrooms, two baths, a garage, and enough property to park our outdoor vehicles. He took notes, and in a week, he had a few houses to show us. So he came by, picked us up, and we drove around looking at houses.

We walked through each and found that each one would need to be remodeled a little bit to work better for us. After the last house he had, he said to us, "Well, that's it. I don't have any other houses to show you right now." Then he paused. "Oh wait, do you guys have a few more minutes?"

We said we did, so he started driving and told us about this other place. "It isn't even on the market yet, but I sold the house right behind this house, and the owners of this house wanted me to come over and give them some ideas of what they needed to do to sell theirs."

We drove to Red Mountain, which is just outside of West Richland; and as we drove by, we liked the way it looked—the house, the yard, and the extra land to park our stuff. This was a manufactured house on an acre of land. About two-thirds of the property was landscaped, and the other remaining one-third was bare land.

As we drove by and turned around to drive by again, the owner of the house (Pam) called Barry on the phone. "Barry, is that you driving in front of my house?"

"Yes, Pam. I was showing some clients your house."

"Well, bring them in! Paul is outside, talk to him for a minute. I'll be right out."

Barry answered her, "Okay, will do." So we pulled into the driveway.

We found Paul, the owner, outside working on a little shed in the back, and we talked to him for a minute and introduced ourselves. He showed us around the property. They had an aboveground swimming pool that was all fenced in and a breezeway in between the house and the garage. We had been there about five minutes when Pam came outside and invited us in, and we went in through the back door into the laundry room. The minute I walked into the house, I knew it was the house that was meant for us. I could feel God's Holy Spirit so strong it almost knocked me over. We walked through the house, but the first time I walked through, I really didn't see it. It was the land, the parking, the landscaping, the pool, and now the house that had me sold, and I was almost overwhelmed. I was captivated by the charming little house that had three bedrooms, two bathrooms, and a garage, and was on an acre of land. It was exactly what we needed.

I told Kery later that we had to go look at it again because I didn't see it the first time. I also told him I really felt like this was the house we were supposed to buy and asked what he thought. And he liked the house but didn't feel as strongly as I felt. We went again and really looked at the house this time. That's when Kery said, "Yes, I like it."

The price was right, so we made an offer. They accepted it, and we had ourselves a new house, with a garage and the land we needed to park all our boats, campers, fifth wheel, and trailers. It really was exactly what we needed to get us out of all the storage units, the fifth wheel, and into a house.

Oz at Forty

Today as I write, my son, Oz, is forty years old and living in Richland, Washington. He works for the same company Kery and I worked for until we retired. In fact, my last years of working, Oz and I worked in the same building. We have had lots of good talks, and Oz told me he found Jesus. After all his injuries and broken bones, he is sore and sits in the hot tub every morning. One day, he was in the hot tub, and he asked God what was going on in his life and why he hadn't just died from all his injuries. God told him, *I am saving you for me.* And then he told him, *And I am saving you from yourself.* He is attending a church created for people who are not comfortable going to a traditional church. The pastor is a pastor's son and does a good job of taking care of lost souls.

Oz is still a wild soul and loves to get out there and live. I admire that about him. He still has no fear and never has really. We all have our problems as we get older, and he seems to be having his share. But he has a good heart, and he tries.

Unfortunately, Oz and Olivia were divorced, and Briar lives predominately with her mom, who has remarried and had another baby with her new husband. Briar will be seven in a few months and is a little spitfire, just like her daddy.

Winslow Jane Smith—Fourth Granddaughter (October 18, 2018)

Olivia remained close to me and Kery because of Briar after she and Oz divorced. Olivia felt her mommy clock ticking and knew she wanted more children. So after about a year, she started dating and finally met a guy named Kevin that she fell in love with. They dated for quite a few months before deciding to get married. It only took Olivia a couple of months, and she was pregnant with Winslow Jane (Winnie). Winnie is still a baby, but she is the cutest little redheaded, blue-eyed baby girl. I can't wait to get to know her better. She lives in Tri-Cities with her mom and dad. Olivia and Kevin make a good couple. They bought a new house, and they are fixing it up the way they want it. Briar has some girls her age who live right next door, so that is a wonderful blessing. Briar is a very good big sister to Winne and loves her greatly.

Retirement Plans

Kery and I worked in Tri-Cities, Washington, until our last working days. We lived "temporarily" in Washington for nine years. He ended up managing the asbestos program for the company we both worked for, and I was an executive assistant for upper management.

I loved my work and my manager Charles and was blessed by my last years of working. Charles was one year younger than Oz. He was smart, young, and active and was a great manager not just for me but for everyone in his group. He truly cared, and this was one of the reasons I appreciated him so much. He made me a better person than I was when I started. We talked like friends, and I served him cheerfully. I actually enjoyed going to work every day. The group of people I worked with were great, and the building we worked in was in town. I was home in fifteen minutes.

Charles's wife, Kendra, had a daughter named Claire, who was the same age as my granddaughter Briar. Kendra got pregnant, and they knew it was boy. His name would be Kyle. One day Charles came into my office and told me that the latest ultrasound of the baby showed he had a dark spot on his lungs. Charles and Kendra were both worried, and as he told me this, my heart was breaking. I knew immediately what I had to do, and that was to pray. I asked Charles if he minded if I prayed for the baby, and he said he didn't. I prayed that God would touch and heal little Kyle and remove or shrink that spot. When I finished and looked up, Charles had his head bowed and his eyes closed. He said thank-you, and there were tears welling up in his eyes.

Kendra had her baby Kyle, and they took him to a specialty doctor in Seattle, Washington, several times. The dark spot is shrinking as he gets older, and the doctors are down to looking at it once a year! I praise God for this and thank him. I think Charles is thankful to him too. I try to see Charles, Kendra, Claire, and Kyle when we go visit Tri-Cities, Washington.

We hadn't planned on working at Hanford and staying in Tri-Cities that long, but God blessed us with jobs that enabled us to pay off our bills and actually retire.

We met so many wonderful people in Tri-Cities and made lots of lifelong friends. We attended a very Holy Spirit-filled church called LifeChurch7 and greatly enjoyed our time there. Our two granddaughters live in Tri-Cities, so we make the trip often to see them, see our friends, and go to church!

Swan Valley, Idaho, and La Ventana, BCS, Mexico

When we got close to our retirement date, we knew we wanted to go back to Idaho, but we had sold our house, our cabin, and did not have any land there at all. Kery started looking for acreage to buy and found a two-and-a-half-acre lot in Swan Valley, Idaho. Swan Valley is where we had our first date floating the river, and it is also where we got married in 1987. Acquiring land in that beautiful valley was a blessing for us both. We bought a beautiful manufactured home to put on our property in Swan Valley and hope to spend our winters in Baja.

We are also happy to find that Kery's best friend Marshall and his wife, Joanne, whom he lived with when we were separated, found us by an old e-mail address a few years ago after being out of touch for quite a few years. Come to find out, they have a cabin in Swan Valley less than five miles from us. We are excited to be reconnected with them with different goals and under different circumstances.

God has blessed our lives abundantly, and I am sure it is because our goal has always been to keep our eyes on Jesus. He is our everything.

We always knew that when we finally retired and spent winters in Baja, we would have some sort of ministry to the people here. We did not know what it was, but we soon found out.

We attended a small gathering of about twenty "gringos" every Sunday called the Fruit of the Spirit Fellowship at Kris and John's house. They did a great job of leading us.

Then one Sunday, they said they had sold their house and were moving to Florida. Many looked to us to take over the leadership, and we prayed about it. About three weeks later, we knew we were supposed to take over the leadership of the Fruit of the Spirit Fellowship.

We also know there will be some sort of ministry in Swan Valley, Idaho, but we have not been there long enough to find out. But we are excited to see what God will do.

Who Is Jesus?

Maybe you have never encountered Jesus and really don't know if you believe in him. I guess I was in the same boat at one time. I always believed in God, but I didn't know or understand about Jesus until my friend Debbie told me that I might know about him but don't know him. The pamphlet she gave me explained it all.

God is holy, and man is sinful. Romans 3:23 says that all of us have sinned compared to the holiness of God. So we were separated from our Holy God. But God loved us so much he sent his Son, Jesus, to pay for our sins so we would not be separated from him.

In John 14:6, Jesus said, "I am the way, the truth and the life. No one comes to the Father except through me." It's impossible for humans to save themselves. We are told that all we have to do is believe that Jesus died for our sins and accept that grace and forgiveness as a free gift. We can't pay for it. It is a gift, and all we have to do is accept his gift of sacrifice for us. By confessing with our mouths that we believe he paid for our sins by dying in our place and that he was resurrected, we are saved and have eternal life. That is the basics of Christianity. Here is a diagram I found online that explains it in a picture.

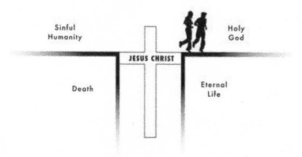

If you would like eternal life and be saved from your sins, all you have to do is say this prayer:

> Dear Lord God, I want to be a part of your family. You said in your Word that if I acknowledge that you raised Jesus from the dead and that I accept Him as my Lord and Savior, I would be saved. Lord, I now confess with my mouth that I do believe you raised Jesus from the dead and that he was resurrected and is alive. I accept him now as my personal Lord and Savior. Amen!

All my life, all I ever wanted was love and acceptance. I was almost dead from the lack of love and acceptance. The darkness was overwhelming. Jesus reached into my coffin and said, "Oh no you don't! I love you, and from now on, it won't matter that they didn't love you." He offered his helping hand to me, and I stepped out of the darkness of my coffin into the light, and my whole life changed.

Sometimes I want to know why. Why they didn't love their children—specifically, why didn't they love me? What they did affected the lives of four innocent victims. But thankfully, I've come to the place where *why* doesn't matter anymore. I am loved and accepted by the Lord, and that's all that matters.

Nine Years Old—A Poem by Patsy Secrist

I was just a little girl
Childlike in every way
What you did changed my life
And took my innocence away

It all started one stormy night
Thunder and lightning
booming outside
I was frightened by the storm
I searched for comfort
by your side

I didn't understand
Why you touched me
that way
I knew it wasn't right
But I didn't know
what to say

Why is this happening
I reasoned to myself
It must be a mistake
But then it happened
again and again
And sadly I found out
that hearts really can
break

MY LOVING DADDY

Hot tears rolled down my cheeks
I just didn't know what to do
Why would you do that to me?
Was the question I held on to

Searching for love to fill my heart
I grew up feeling
damaged
and used
As good men came and went,
You were always
the great excuse

Trust doesn't come easy for me
I've taken it one day at a time
Finally, Jesus came and healed my heart
And I forgave you for your crime

Thank you, Jesus, for saving my life
My heart longed
for a loving embrace
I gave you my broken heart
And you gave me
true love and grace

Forgiveness does not come easy
But it is without a doubt
The thing to do
Because if you never do it
Precious one
You are the one to lose

"My Story," a song by Big Daddy Weave

From the album *Beautiful Offerings*
Song written by Mike Weaver and Jason Ingram

If I told you my story
You would hear hope that wouldn't let go
If I told you my story
You would hear love that never gave up
If I told you my story
You would hear life but it wasn't mine

If I should speak then let it be

Of the grace that is greater than all my sin
Of when justice was served and where mercy wins
Of the kindness of Jesus that draws me in
To tell you my story is to tell of Him

If I told you my story
You would hear victory over the enemy
If told you my story
You would hear freedom that was won for me
If I told you my story
You would hear life overcome the grave

If I should speak then let it be—this is my story
This is my song praising my Savior all the day long

Hannah's Prayer

My heart rejoices in the LORD! The LORD has made me strong. Now I have an answer for my enemies; I rejoice because you rescued me. No one is holy like the LORD! There is on one besides you: there is no Rock like our God! (1 Samuel 2:1, 2)

"Goodness of God," a song by Jenn Johnson and Bethel Music

I love You, Lord
For Your mercy never failed me
All my days, I've been held in Your hands
From the moment that I wake up
Until I lay my head
Oh, I will sing of the goodness of God
And all my life You have been faithful
And all my life You have been so, so good
With every breath that I am able
Oh, I will sing of the goodness of God
I love Your voice
You have led me through the fire
And in darkest night You are close like no other
I've known You as a Father
I've known You as a Friend
And I have lived in the goodness of God, yeah!
And all my life You have been faithful, ohh
And all my life You have been so, so good
With every breath that I am able
Oh, I will sing of the goodness of God, yeah!
'Cause Your goodness is running after, it's running after me
Your goodness is running after, it's running after me
With my life laid down, I'm surrendered now
I give You everything
'Cause Your goodness is running after, it's running after me, oh-ohh

'Cause Your goodness is running after, it's running after me
Your goodness is running after, it's running after me
With my life laid down, I'm surrendered now
I give You everything
'Cause Your goodness is running after, it keeps running after me
And all my life You have been faithful
And all my life You have been so, so good
With every breath that I am able
Oh, I'm gonna sing of the goodness of God
I'm gonna sing, I'm gonna sing
'Cause all my life You have been faithful
And all my life You have been so, so good
With every breath that I am able
Oh, I'm gonna sing of the goodness of God
Oh, I'm gonna sing of the goodness of God

Final Prayer

Father God, I come before you now to pray for every person who reads this book. Each one of them are created by you and are called by your name. Lord, I pray for each of them, that they will pray and receive your Holy Spirit. I pray that you will live in their hearts, and they will know you are there. May they feel your glorious and unconditional love that has no end.

I pray that your Holy Spirit within them will give them strength to accomplish whatever they set out to do. Lord, you are trustworthy, you are wonderful, you give us all that we will ever need, and we know that with you, nothing is impossible!

Father, I give you praise, and I worship your most Holy Name. Abba, Papa, Father, Daddy, I will forever be grateful for your love in my heart. I thank you with all that I have for saving me and giving me this life abundant. You are so personal, so close, so awesome, so caring, so wonderful, so thoughtful, so good to me. You are everything to me. You are my loving Daddy.

About the Author

Patsy is a delightful person who knows who she is—a precious daughter of the King of kings, and she lives her life accordingly. She is a vivacious woman of God who has been radically transformed by the hearing of just one important phrase from the Lord. She follows where the Lord leads her and devotes her life to lifting others up. She loves people and fosters community everywhere she goes. She has led women's Bible study groups and deeply loves her friends. May her victorious life story be an encouragement to you as you share in her journey to freedom and joy.